The Emerging New Age

The Emerging New Age

by J.L. Simmons Ph.D.

LIBRARY OF CONGRESS CATALOGING-IN-PUBLICATION DATA

Simmons, J.L. (Jerry Laird), 1933—
The emerging new age / by J.L. Simmons.
p. cm.
Bibliography: p.
ISBN 0-939680-65-3 :
1. New Age movement. 2. Occultism. 3. Psychic Research.
I. Title.
BP605.N48S55 1989
133—dc20 89-34213
CIP

Bear & Company
Santa Fe, New Mexico 87504-2860

Cover and interior design: Kathleen Katz
Typography: Buffalo Publications
Printed in the United States of America by R.R. Donnelley

9 8 7 6 5 4 3 2 1

Contents

Acknowledgements

Everything has contributed to this book. I wish to thank my preternatural editors, Nola Simmons, Barbara Clow, Harriet Slavitz, and Gail Vivino for their wonderful midwifing. Also Kathleen Katz and Debora Bluestone for their book design and promotion. And the rest of the Bear Clan for being there. Never before have I had such a positive publishing experience, and this is the understatement of the week.

Gratitude to my wife, Nola, and my two sons, Christopher and David, for all I've learned from them.

I thank my lucky stars for my typist, Jennine Bosecker, who performed at a level above the mundane.

And I wish to acknowledge and warmly thank all the Pathfinders. With few signposts and little or no support they ventured into unknown territories to blaze the trails that have made the New Age a possibility. My book is only one of the many monuments to them that are now springing up everywhere.

Prologue

What's *really* going on in this world is very different from what *appears* to be going on, as expressed in newspaper headlines or in conventional textbooks. I knew something was stirring in the world but I didn't know what. There was something "in the air" that was not being mentioned on the six o'clock news—something tantalizing. I knew it wasn't in the college textbooks because I taught these courses. I asked other professionals in my network, but they didn't know either. Well, I was a trained and experienced researcher; I'd find out for myself.

There was another thing. Off and on throughout my life I have had "funny experiences" that couldn't be explained by any of the theories I learned while earning my doctorate in social psychology. They simply didn't fit into mainstream intellectual worldviews or the conventional Judeo-Christian belief systems. At the same time I kept running into ordinary people who were telling me about the very extraordinary experiences *they* were having. Through the years this continued to happen both in my personal life and in my field research interviews on youth culture, deviance, relationships, whatever. Most of these people were entirely untutored in any mystical or parapsychological literature. When they asked me the meaning of their unexplainable experiences I could only shrug and say, "I don't know."

Somewhere along the line the suspicion grew within me that the "something in the air" and these "funny experiences" of mine and others were connected. I asked myself, "What's going on here?" I decided to go looking for books that might offer some insight, and to go talk with some more people.

Books, books, books; people, people, people. Whole new worlds opened up to me. I found many good books and many good people. And I discovered nothing less than a worldwide spiritual awakening.

There were, it turned out, millions of people more or less involved in an amorphous, unofficial "movement" just a couple of steps off to the side of mainstream society. I recalled that throughout history most breakthroughs and transformations had made their first appearance on the fringes of society.

I found enough books on the supernatural, psychic experiences, past lives, journeys beyond this world, and spiritual awakenings to strain the shelf capacity of any public library. They seemed to vary greatly in quality, clarity, and user-friendliness. There were books written by philosophers, religionists, scientists of one kind or another, occultists, and "New Age" researchers and practitioners. But I couldn't find the book I was looking for.

Among all of these shelves and roomfuls of writings, I found the new researchers and practitioners to be far and away the most useful and most directly relevant to the unusual experiences of myself and others. They also seemed to be the most in tune with current situations, predicaments, and possibilities. (No doubt the older books had been in tune with their times.) Among the contemporary spiritual books and people I found some answers that added up to a verifiable fantastic story. And I found that they too knew there was something in the air.

I had one problem with the contemporary books. Most of them were specialized, dealing with only one aspect of what was going on, such as near-death experiences, or astral travel, or reincarnation, or communication from the Beyond. I wanted to know the overall *pattern*, the composite emerging portrait. A good many people, starting out from different places, seemed to be heading in the same direction. But how did all these separate strands fit together? I decided to write the book I had been looking for.

My purpose has been to synthesize what I have read and seen and experienced; to weave the exciting new developments together into a coherent picture. I wanted to present this picture without offering endless proofs or engaging in unseemly debates with those who do not wish to look.

I don't believe anyone would call me an enlightened person. I live in the world and my problems and pleasures are not much different from anyone else abiding here. I am a social psychologist, field researcher, and writer by profession, and an explorer and outrider by inclination.

I am not a spiritual leader, nor am I a devotee of any special discipline or cult. I do not make my living through any psychic practice. So I have no vested interest in any particular Way.

I approach the writing of this book with a great deal of humility. The cosmos is vast to say the least. So at best I'm a sort of first-grader telling preschoolers about some glimpses of the larger neighborhood. But I'm not a bully or a know-it-all. And I've done a lot of homework on these subjects.

The personal journey involved in producing this book provided many realizations for me; and I hope it may provide some for you. If not, it may at least provide some provocations.

At bottom this book is an invitation. While reading it you might change your mind, and, as so many mystics, old and new, have said, if you change your mind you change your future.

1

The Emerging Spiritual Awakening

Personal lives and social conditions are far more fluid than we usually realize. Think how different you were ten years ago. Think how different you will probably be ten years from now. Whether we like it or not, whether we are even aware of it, we are presently in the midst of a transition to a new era. We can't go back. And what we go forward *to* seems to be largely in our own hands. That fact is enough to make just about everyone a bit nervous.

You won't find out much about this transition from our current textbooks because they pertain mostly to a world that is already fading and they hardly mention our probable futures. You won't learn much about it from any of our planet's official leaders because it is still "unofficial." These textbook writers and leaders are not necessarily bad or stupid; it's just that they are *official* representatives of the old order.

This distinction between official and unofficial is important. In the early 1950s, Alfred Kinsey and his associates startled the world by presenting evidence that a significant percentage of Americans were engaging in sexual practices that were not acknowledged or even recognized by our official culture. In the mid-fifties a brash new unofficial music began to emerge. "Decent" radio stations wouldn't play it and it was not taken very seriously — except by the millions of people who were buying the records. Meanwhile, around the country, kids who would become international stars in a few years were plunking away in basements and garages, learning to play their guitars. In both these cases, few would have guessed what was to follow. Not many Romans took Christianity very seriously, either.

So far, the new spiritual awakening movement is not being taken very seriously in contemporary official circles. A few reporters have been sent out to do tongue-in-cheek stories; a few Establishment doctors and scientists have made derisive pronouncements about it; many, but not all, churchmen have condemned it as counterfeit and demonic; the academic community has largely ignored it and withheld research funding; and it provides joke material for comedians and cartoonists. Meanwhile, millions of people are, in one way or another, becoming *unofficially* involved in it.

The signs of the new movement are everywhere, if one wishes to look. Researchers are finding an abundance of cases of transforming mystical experiences among people revived after being clinically dead. A national opinion poll shows that the number of Americans believing in past lives has increased from about one-seventh to one-fourth of the population in the last dozen years. A store selling spiritual books and paraphernalia opens in a small midwestern city and does a thriving business from the first day. Paperback books on various aspects of the paranormal are continuing to go through printing after printing, which means that *someone* is buying them. Nobel Prize-winning scientists are quoting ancient Buddhist tracts and writing articles that go beyond most science fiction in their cosmic premises and implications. A little shoestring psychic magazine grows into a circulation of over one-hundred-fifty thousand within five years. During in-depth interviews, a majority of widows report spirit visitations from their deceased spouses and add that they don't dare tell their doctors. A growing legion of past-life regression therapists are alleviating conditions which had stubbornly resisted conventional therapeutic and medical treatments. In the wake of mounting dissatisfaction with some of the questionable practices of conventional medicine, there is a groundswell movement toward alternative health technologies. Streamlined, westernized yoga classes are popping up across the land and the techniques are being extended to include the elderly and disabled. A Miami sociologist transforms many students' lives by teaching them to love other people, such as shut-ins, who they would ordinarily never have looked at twice. A Virginia institute is producing altered states of consciousness by using controlled sound to teach people to integrate the left and right hemispheres of their brains. And so on, and so on.

Here's an interesting thought. Using the available data, a statistician friend and I have estimated that, while you are reading this book, at any time, over one-million other people in the world are also reading some book on spiritual development. You have company.

All these signs of spiritual awakening still involve only a fraction of the populace. But over the last decade this minority has shown a growth rate that would be the envy of any new corporation. New people become involved in some aspect of this spiritual awakening movement each day. This growth is also cumulative, because a great many interviews have verified that once people begin some kind of spiritual journey they may take time out to rest or recoup, but very few of them ever cease to quest entirely. After analyzing data from England and America, Peter Russell, the noted British visionary physicist, estimates that the human potential movement is doubling in size every three to five years.

The mass media have picked up the package label "New Age" for this diverse spiritual movement. So far, their coverage has usually not been very informative, focusing mainly on the most superficial and sensational aspects of what's really going on. The quieter, stronger, more deep-running aspects are almost entirely missed in their hasty reportage. They are not entirely to blame for this; if I went to an unfamiliar country, say Thailand, for a few days, my subsequent report would also no doubt be superficial and would miss most of the real situation there. You couldn't find out much about Thailand from me.

The media do recognize that something is happening. But *why* is it happening? Why are people following new directions? For each of the individuals who become involved, the reasons lie within his or her personal story. However, there does seem to be something of a more general answer. In our time of present uncertainties and future shocks, when our -ologies and -isms no longer seem to fit our experience very well, a good many people are searching. Ironically, the very same civilization that has created our turmoils and unrests has also set up the conditions for the New Age to arise. Researchers, using the best of science, have followed their data trails to uncover and begin to map the spiritual nature of human beings and the incredible aliveness of All That Is. Their findings have been integrated with the messages left by ancient mystics and the hints and intuitions of pioneer investigators. This unique creative fusion promises to give us a clearer and more exciting idea of the real nature of physical and spiritual life than we have ever had before.

For many people this emerging picture has already shown its ability to calm and revitalize and give back hope, to provide some direction and some dreams. And to change lives.

It's beginning to look like this portrayal might well be "the inside story" of life on this planet and beyond. If so, this may currently be the most vital information in the world, with incredible implications for every man, woman, and child alive today. For certain, the picture offered is much more exciting and uplifting than the ones offered in mainstream medical and psychology texts. What more can you ask of an unfinished portrait?

A New Age Manifesto

As one delves into the strands which comprise the emerging New Age pattern, there might at first seem to be a bewildering swirl of reported experiences, interpretations, theories, and borrowed dogmas that threatens to be endless. But, happily, as one continues to search and sift through all of this, a few central themes common to almost all lines of approach emerge. These themes are the basic premises of the spiritual awakening movement.

If you find some of these premises to be bothersome and in gross opposition to your own present beliefs, please don't just throw the book into your garage sale bin — read on. Some of these ideas can take some getting used to. If you're not presently involved in the movement, you will at least discover something about what "those people" are thinking and doing, and that there is rapidly growing empirical evidence to support their assertions. The implications are nothing less than world-changing. Here they are:

— Every human being has a spiritual essence which, no matter how buried at the moment, is the living force, the "I" within each individual. Consciousness is not some by-product of biological processes; instead, biological forms are ultimately manifestations of consciousness. The body doesn't "have a soul"; rather, the soul temporarily has a body.

— At present, most people identify very strongly with and become immersed in the material world (physical plane) like avid fans hypnotically entranced within a game. There is nothing necessarily wrong with materialistic pursuits, as such: they can provide us with learning experiences and adventure. But when they are coupled with utter neglect or denial of spiritual realities, this can create a life that is unbalanced and impeded in its development. Consider this: many people who spend more than an hour a day grooming their bodies sincerely believe that they have no time for spiritual pursuits. This is not a condemnation; just a pointer.

— Currently, most people are spiritual sleepwalkers — largely unaware, even comatose as spiritual beings. During waking hours this includes a state of virtual amnesia regarding their true nature and heritage, although this nature comes alive during some sleep states. Ordinarily these experiences are poorly remembered, if at all, upon waking.

— At present, most people are therefore largely unaware of how spiritual influences affect our daily lives, and of our psychic interaction with the world around us. These nonphysical influences occur continuously, whether we are conscious of them or not.

— All paranormal experiences and psychic abilities stem directly from the nature of the spirit or soul. We call these events "supernatural," but, in fact, they are some of the most natural things that spirits do. Focused on the physical plane as we are, when these events occur we tend to ignore them, or explain them away as coincidence and imagination. Also, until very recently we greatly underestimated how widespread such experiences were, because people were hesitant to talk about them publicly. This is changing.

— Spiritual matters are far more important than most people realize. Many people conceive of the spiritual realms, if they even grant their existence, as shadowy and intangible compared with the "real" and immediate bustle of daily living. But the evidence points to the spiritual realms being more basic and permanent and less illusory than the physical plane. Many believe the physical universe will exist long after we are gone, when, in truth, we will exist long after the physical universe is gone.

— The cosmos is brimming over with spiritual life. There are very real spiritual or astral planes which are not vague, drab places, but rich and colorful beyond description. There the spirit can experience 1001 sensations and emotions far beyond the common lot of incarnate humanity. There the spirit also experiences "expanded consciousness"; the blinders are removed, as it were. These astral realms are sometimes travelled in dreams, visited in near-death experiences and other transcendent states, and inhabited after physical death. According to many accounts, this is where "the good times are."

— Individually and collectively, we create the realities we experience. This is the essence of "karma". Our beliefs, positive or negative, limiting or affirming, create reality. This is the basis of the various Creative Visualization techniques. Ordinarily, beliefs remain largely unexamined and out of conscious control. Jose Silva, the originator of Silva Mind Control, describes the uncontrolled mind as a drunken monkey lurching from thought to thought.

— There are a great many levels of consciousness or spiritual awareness. Humans vary greatly in these qualities, and disembodied spirits vary even more. Beings of similar consciousness levels tend to associate with one another on the basis of "Like Attracts Like." This includes the vitally important corollary that beings can increase their own awareness and can aid others in consciousness expansion.

— Effort and self-discipline are needed in order to rise to higher levels of spiritual awareness and understanding, especially if a person wishes to accelerate the natural growth process. This need not involve denial, asceticism, or withdrawal from active living, but it does necessarily involve some work.

— There are traps, frauds, misdirections, self-delusions, and addictions to look out for as one walks a spiritual path. None of these are ultimately fatal to the spiritual being, but they can produce needless anguish and unhappiness. It is important to learn to be a knowledgeable and savvy traveller, to stay independent, and to listen to one's own intuitional guides. As Robert Monroe so forcefully points out in *Far Journeys*, physical-plane living, with its games and goals, its survival and sex preoccupations, is highly addictive. Enjoy, but don't get hooked!

— All human beings are involved in the process of evolving spiritually, whether we presently recognize and accept this fact or not. The fact of this evolution is inevitable and inescapable, but how hard or easy the process will be is, to a large degree, in our own hands. This is Earth School; the physical plane is our present schoolroom (complete with recess periods) and we cannot in the long run dodge or cheat on the lessons we are here to learn. More highly evolved spirits assist us in our endeavors, but free choice always remains with us. As the discarnate teacher, Michael, says in *Messages From Michael* (Chelsea Quinn Yarbro, scribe), we can learn the easy way or the hard way, but we will learn eventually.

— We are all connected, physically and spiritually. Our feelings of separateness, aloneness, and alienation are negative distortions of this fact. As the visionary ecologist, Barbara Ward noted, we are all crew members of "Spaceship Earth," dependent upon and responsible for its life-support systems. Spiritually, we are each independent, yet simultaneously an inseparable part of All That Is. We are, underneath it all, companions on the road.

These premises add up to a sort of manifesto of the spiritual awakening movement. This might all seem like cold comfort to someone languishing in a Central American prison, or a woman on her own, trying to raise two children on a subsistence salary. It might also seem irrelevant to a young, upwardly mobile professional who is on a good roll in his or her career and relationships. But perhaps such situations only demonstrate how stuck and off course we can get. The bottom-line assertion of the New Age is that things don't have to be the way they are. There are other possibilities, as we will see.

2

Psychic Influences

Our apparently mundane physical reality floats upon a sea of psychic events and influences. These continuous occurrences are so subtle that, if one's focus is entirely on the physical plane, they are almost always missed. But they are still there — influencing everything.

By far the greatest number of paranormal incidents are of a subliminal nature, close to the surface of awareness but not consciously realized. You have an uneasy feeling about a friend, who turns out, in fact, to be in trouble. You are spontaneously drawn to the homey atmosphere of a house, rent it, and have an enjoyable time living there. You get good grades in some particular subject with next to no effort because it just "comes naturally" to you. While idly fooling around, you correctly call the hidden faces of four or five cards in a row, then try again seriously and fail. You have a strong feeling you should leave a party early, and you'll never know if you averted some mishap or danger because you did leave. You call a loved one only to hear, "I was just thinking of calling you!" A senior citizen falls in love again and spontaneously recovers her health, to the utter puzzlement of her doctors. A veteran nurse has unusually high releases from intensive care, while the patients of another nurse routinely show poor and slow recoveries. When a troublesome relative comes to visit, sinks stop up and appliances break down for no apparent reason, then run again when that person leaves. One person has a green thumb, another is good with animals, cranky machinery will always run for someone else. *Such things are occurring all around us on a daily basis; whether we realize it or not, we are continually bathed in the psychic medium.*

These things are like extreme peripheral vision, something half-sensed out of the corner of one's eye. Yet there is another category of "supernatural" happenings which are a bit more discernable. If you talk to anyone long enough, perhaps in the late evening or over a beer, you'll usually find a curious thing. Touch upon the paranormal a few times and your companion will almost certainly begin to tell you stories of the uncanny, involving themselves or their acquaintances: stories about an aunt who dreamed her son was hurt the night before he actually was; about an overwhelming sense of familiarity with some place they visited for the first time; about knowing on first meeting that they were going to marry a certain person; of a cat who always jumped in their lap and purred when they felt bad; of swearing they felt their grandfather's presence just after he died, and so on. The next day, over cafeteria lunch, these same people will have "returned to normal" and be fully focused on what they consider the real world.

If you explore further, you will find another curious thing. A large number of people are quietly engaging in spiritual or mystical pursuits and embracing beliefs that, if revealed, would astonish their co-workers, clients, and acquaintances. These people come from all stations in life; they may be department store clerks and gardeners, prison guards, locally established professionals, journal editors, celebrities. The person sitting next to you in a restaurant might well be involved in some very esoteric pursuits in his or her spare time. For example, I know a well-established dentist who found his wife of many years through a spontaneous psychic homing, who anonymously gives financial aid to several occult groups in his area, and who goes into a meditative trance to "chat" with his sister who resides several thousand miles away.

As an off-the-cuff experiment, just to see what would happen, I casually mentioned psychic phenomena in a noncommital fashion to ten small groups of people. These were groups varying in size from two to seven persons with whom I had a mild acquaintance, and they were from the Midwest, the bastion of conventionality. The results were startling. In every one of the ten groups, some of the people began telling stories of psychic experiences that had happened to them or someone they knew well. The stories were pretty much the standard ones, such as that of a woman who suddenly knew when her distant sister died and felt her brief visiting presence telling her not to worry or mourn. Or the Vietnam veteran who followed a strong premonition and lied his way out of a mission which did, in fact, turn out to be a massacre. Or a nurse telling of a patient who felt she had died during surgery, gone to a beautiful loving place, and come back; the patient was no longer afraid of death, but was afraid to tell anybody. In six of the ten groups there was also mention of some friend or relative who was a serious devotee of some spiritual discipline. There was a fairly strong consensus among those in each group that, "there's something to all this kind of stuff, but who knows what?" They were far more certain about the validity of the incidents than about what they might mean.

My own informal interview results are certainly not unique. Every researcher has found larger numbers of people having direct experiences with the supernatural than any previous official estimates suggested. Psychic experiences, we must conclude, are very common. So we have very widespread experience with the paranormal among the populace, coupled with an official mainstream society which denies the existence or the spiritual nature of such things. An interesting paradox, which cannot hold for long. Note that the people in my little experiment would not be considered New Age by others or themselves.

A very large proportion of the tingles, buzzes, flushes, sexual thrills, tensions, and good feelings we experience are the result of incoming spiritual impingements from others. We continually bathe in a swirl of telepathic images and vibrations from those around us. And we, of course, are continually broadcasting our own vibrations and images to others, near and far. All of this cacophony is almost entirely uncontrolled and usually unrecognized at a conscious level. As Robert Monroe has pointed out, this forms a "noise background" to physical-plane living which can be almost overwhelming, for example, in the downtown areas of large cities. This is one reason why wilderness retreats can sometimes be so restful. By simply paying more attention, one can become more sensitive to and aware of these incoming influences.

The universal psychic interconnections among beings are convincingly demonstrated for those who wish to look at all the sorts of resonances we experience with others. Such resonances are felt as harmonious or dissonant vibrations of support, friendliness, attraction, cheerfulness or disapproval, "rubbing the wrong way," sulkiness, viciousness, and so on. We pick up on these vibrations, and our own moods and actions can be heavily influenced by them.

If someone wishes you ill or is actively hating you, this can create a feeling of malaise. If someone else feels very warm toward and supportive of you, this can provide a buoyant, upbeat current to help carry you through the day. Your interpersonal network is an important determinant of the "climate" within which you move. You have, of course, co-authored this network along with its other members.

At the group level, we have the psychic atmosphere of a gathering, a crowd, or a neighborhood, and the organization where we work. Families have their own collective auras, as do schools and sports teams and music groups, that can be sensed by members and sensitive observers.

I well remember myself as a lonely pockmarked teenager, walking into a lounge where a student clique hung out and being suddenly washed over with waves of exuberance. Moments later I was told by the half dozen clique members that a girl, not there, really liked me and wanted me to take her to the prom. These sorts of incidents can be the memorabilia of a lifetime.

In *The Aquarian Conspiracy*, Marilyn Ferguson has pointed out that, in human relationships, one plus one never equals two; the combination is always more or less than two. It's our spiritual natures and spiritual interconnections that upset the logical left-brain arithmetic.

Any human relationship has both a physical and a spiritual component. These two components may be complementary, which makes for a lot of harmonious living, but they can also conflict with one another.

On the physical-plane level, social scientists have documented how we relate to one another through such factors as physical proximity, network acquaintanceships, and similarity in social class and interests. People such as co-workers, travelling companions, and fellow students — thrown together by circumstances — become friends and maybe spouses. Also, we usually feel warmly toward those who assist us in our physical-plane games and cooly toward those who impede us, whatever the psychic resonances might be.

But then there are also affinities that are more completely spiritual. These go beyond relationships of convenience. Real togetherness, camaraderie, and intimacy are spiritually based. Real enmity and vindictiveness that go beyond what the facts might seem to warrant are also spiritually based. Grand passions rise above and beyond simple physical-plane facts, whether they are consuming loves or "an eye for an eyelash" hatreds.

If the mundane and spiritual components of affinity coincide, a double-bonding can occur, resulting in a deep and abiding attachment, able to stand up to most vicissitudes. However, if the two components are discrepant, there is likely to be trouble, at least inside the head of the person experiencing the discrepancy. Each component can overrule the other. Someone may feel strong spiritual affinities with another but pass that person by because of circumstances, previous commitments, or other plans. Or someone may disregard and abandon existing mundane commitments because he or she is overwhelmed and carried away by the sheer force of a discovered spiritual affinity. I've seen it happen both ways. This is the stuff of great literature and music, whether tragic or exuberant. Spiritual relationships have often shown their ability to cut across age, social class, race, nationality, or any other physical plane barriers. They are most likely to be ignored and denied by those deeply entranced in the physical plane.

The seemingly cosmic law of Like Attracts Like leads humans to seek their own spiritual level within the surrounding social order during any given lifetime. More precisely, this is a process of an individual attracting and being attracted into relationships and situations involving persons of similar vibration or wavelength levels. Friends, couples, families, gangs, and groups, and even communities and tribes, will therefore tend to share particular levels of awareness. It follows that the people involved tend to reinforce one another's spiritual levels. This can simultaneously be both a mutual support and a constraint to keep one at that level.

No one is, of course, stuck at any specific level forever — or I wouldn't be writing this book and you wouldn't be reading it. A person can be "uplifted" through meeting someone at a higher level of evolvement, experiencing art or music, or rising above a crisis: through anything that touches the soul. A person can also be converted to a lower vibrational level through, for example, the brutalization accompanying a long war, or becoming substance addicted, or sexual debauchery. This is the idea of sinking to the level of one's enemy and of being seduced by temptations — what Iris Belhayes, the author of *Spirit Guides: We Are Not Alone*, calls "falling through the cracks." Such a fall is not fatal to any being — nothing is. Nor is it irreversible. And, in the long run, one is not spiritually tainted or soiled as a result. However, the sheer pleasures and sensations available at the higher vibrational levels make the game of upward striving exceedingly worthwhile. *Low-vibration-level people are very naive, indeed, when they think high-vibration-level people don't have fun.*

Are there special circumstances that increase the likelihood of psychic experiences reaching full consciousness? At first glance, such occurrences might seem random and haphazard. However, a closer inspection of cases reveals something of a pattern — circumstances where they are more likely to arise. It seems there must be some sort of *triggering* to override a person's physical-plane immersion and clickety-click-click logical thought processes.

Interestingly, there are two extremes of experience in which paranormal happenings are most likely to burst through into awareness: extreme stress conditions on the one hand, and extreme lightheartedness on the other. In the psychological middle ground of rationality and sequential logic, all the evidence indicates they are least likely to occur. This is probably so because both the extremes of dire straits and of high playfulness are likely to connect into spirituality, while rational, reasonable thinking and acting are not.

There are two factors present during extreme stress conditions, such as survival threats or direct threats to the well-being of loved ones: present-time intensity, and the failure of ordinary conventional means to handle the situation. These two factors operating together are sometimes sufficient to impel the individual to rise above and beyond ordinary habits and barriers to call forth spiritual incidents which are consciously experienced.

High-spirited playfulness, in the other extreme, seems also to occasionally disengage the ordinary barriers to psychic awareness. This seems especially to be so when one has nothing to lose and no anxiousness or fear about failure, as when one is playing cards for penny stakes or idly calling up the next card. Several times, both my eldest son and I have offhandedly called four cards in a row. The statistical odds of doing this by chance are one in more than seven million.

Note that laboratory experimental conditions, conducted by rational minded (beta wave) personnel, touch neither of these extreme conditions. This is the main reason why most researchers have left the laboratory and turned instead to naturalistic research approaches, gathering their data directly from the field, like the anthropologists and botanists.

It might be interesting to see if a lighhearted experimenter who clowned around with his subjects would increase laboratory ESP test scores . . . .

There are no doubt other factors which increase the chances of psychic phenomena reaching awareness. An obvious one is the social climate within a family or network in which there is some conscious experience of, and belief in, things spiritual, and where they are not just dismissed as imagination. Growing up in a family or running around with people who freely talk about spiritual experiences and ideas provides a more nurturant atmosphere for having such ideas and experiences oneself. Being raised in a region or culture where these things are accepted is also supportive of such personal experiences and explorations.

The most reliable factor for increasing anyone's awareness of psychic incidents and influences is through achieving a higher level of consciousness. Since all psychic phenomena seem to have their basis in the essential nature of spirits, it follows that the techniques people use to heighten spiritual awareness would also increase conscious recognition of the psychic events occurring around them.

Psychic events are always occurring. It is our *awareness* of them that fluctuates. When a person is deeply focused and actively immersed in the physical plane, the larger spiritual realms seem quite unreal and mostly irrelevant. The pull of physical activities, involvements, and problems can be very strong, even all consuming, as we can all attest. I've seen even professional psychics and mystics get utterly bogged down in the business side of their occupations. A nature-loving friend of mine left college to become a farmer, but found himself so enmeshed in the details of making a go of it that he had little time to enjoy the outdoors he loved so much. Can a good businessman be a mystic; can a mystic be a good businessman? Yes — if they can integrate the two spheres. The "bridges" between physical life and spirituality, between the physical and spiritual planes, seem to be tricky and tenuous ones for most people. People are having "minor" psychic experiences all the time, but these usually go unrecognized or are shrugged off or explained away. In our mainstream society, some physiological or psychological explanation is commonly given for the valid hunch, or the vivid dream, or the uncanny recognition of a person or place. Or it is simply shrugged off with a "who knows?"

For those deeply involved in conventional society, such garden-variety psychic incidents can also be easily clouded over by all the intrusions of the workaday world. The biological routines of the body, the demands of a work schedule, the necessity to go do the laundry, even the ringing of the telephone, can intervene to renew a physical-plane focus. The afterglow of some light brush with the spiritual may last for a while to imbue our chores with a bit of magic (the original meaning of the word glamour), but the glamour tends to fade. Since most people recognize only dimly, if at all, the essential nature of such touches, the fading is hastened and, on a mundane level of awareness, the memories are difficult to recapture. But wisps of remembrance usually remain to haunt a person, at odd times, with reminders that life can be more than the treadmill it may sometimes seem.

Fundamentally, there seems to most people to be an ambivalence between the physical and the spiritual. For example, when far-out claims about the paranormal are made, as with Shirley MacLaine or the Harmonic Convergence, there is a widespread backlash of ridicule and disbelief. But conversely, when spiritual occurrences are condemned as rubbish by some Establishment preacher or scientist, there is a widespread backlash of "well, there's *something* to all these things," followed by a story about some unexplainable experience. And so it goes.

How to bring the two focuses together and integrate them in one's daily life? Not too many people want to become other-worldly mystics. This would probably not even be wise for most people, because their biological units and social connections are here and now. And from all accounts we are here to experience the physical plane. But to live only on the mundane level is at best to be only a crafty brute. There's an old blues song that says: Things go better with a little bit of soul.

3

Some Common Psychic Incidents

There seems to be a great variety of common occurrences which have such a "bit of soul" in them. The following catalogue of paranormal experiences is culled from the direct reports of people I have known or interviewed over the years. I have used descriptive language, reflecting their own words, rather than technical jargon because, as Ingo Swann has pointed out in *Natural ESP*, such technical jargon has buried assumptions which can be more misleading than informative.

Surveys have not told us much about how people balance the spiritual with the mundane in their lives, or what they *think* of paranormal experiences. But, whatever their beliefs, the vast majority of Americans report having had one or more of the following types of experiences, according to national opinion polls.

The sheer range of experiences that have a direct spiritual component to them is much broader than has usually been recognized. And a bit of self-examination might reveal that they are much more common than is ordinarily realized. You may have personally experienced several of them.

— Hunches. Intuitive feelings and flashes about situations or events, which bypass and rise above ordinary logical processes or data gathering. These used to be called subconscious processes, but *superconsciousness* of one sort or another seems to be the actual source. Often we override such feelings and proceed logically; then, when they turn out to have been correct, we say, "I had a hunch about that."

— Directly sensing the moods, emotions, and intentions of other people. Such sensings are often vague and subliminal, but sometimes startlingly sharp and clear. We "pick up on" others continually, often sensing what people are *not* saying, or a big discrepancy between what they are saying and what they really mean. This sensing cannot be merely a matter of observing subtle body language, because we often do it when the other person is not physically present.

— Sensing an accident, sickness, or misfortune befalling some person or pet animal who is physically distant. This is usually, but not always, someone we are intimately involved with. The sensing is strong enough to interrupt our ongoing conscious processes and to override geographical distances.

— Thinking of someone who then immediately phones or writes, perhaps with the remark that a thought about you had come into their mind. Even people who have no truck with the supernatural nor much belief in it will tell you that this sometimes happens to them.

— Sensing the "vibrations" of a physical locale or object such as a house, or neighborhood, or piece of jewelry, without having any previous knowledge about them. The sensed vibrations may be good or bad, happy or foreboding.

— Strongly hoping that something would happen, which then subsequently occurs "as if by magic." This also has the negative side of fearing something which you "just know is going to happen" that does indeed then befall you. Happily, these negative self-fulfilling prophecies can be changed. Read on.

— Sensing unseen presences. Such awareness is "direct": that is, it doesn't involve our physical perception channels. From reports that I have received, I would guess that this experience is very common amongst the current populace. The three main forms reported are: visitation from a relative or loved one who recently died; the sensing of disembodied spirits in a "haunted" house or locale; and the sensing of spirit guides or guardian angels. By using one New Age technique or another, a growing number of people are now becoming adept at deliberately communicating with discarnate beings.

— Inspiration. This is widely acknowledged by writers, artists, and even scientists, and it involves claims of insights stemming from some higher source or guiding force. This also includes the common testimonials about spiritual intervention into peoples' lives during times of trouble or danger.

— Having an uncanny skill or knowledge about some subject. The most outstanding examples of this are child prodigies. Such preternatural abilities are commonly called a "gift" — but what does "gift" mean? Small children with professional-level mathematics, language, or musical abilities simply destroy all of our carefully constructed child-development theories. More frequent examples of this include a swift intuitive grasp of some subject, or the swiftly acquired mastery of a foreign language or the highly literate form of one's own language. If you search long enough, you will find that virtually everyone has such an unexplainable ability.

— Uncanny familiarity with some geographical location you've supposedly never visited before. This one is reported almost routinely by those who travel and vacation extensively.

— Uncanny familiarity with, understanding of, or interest in some previous historical epoch, its culture and costumes, its architecture, rituals, and lifestyles. You can sometimes sense such affinities in the works of certain writers and artists.

— An almost overwhelming feeling of familiarity with a person you've just met, as if you had known each other before. The feelings that go along with this recognition can range from strong instant attraction to strong instant dislike. Various kinds of physical sensations, emotional flushes, and mental stirrings often accompany such meetings.

— Psychic influence upon physical objects. The most striking form of this is the poltergeist phenomenon: the rattling or throwing of physical objects, the tapping of tables, and so on. Milder but much more common manifestations are expressed by those people who have a "magic touch" in working with machinery and mechanical processes. A negative form exists in people who break everything they go near.

— Out-of-body experiences (OOBs). The most dramatic and extensively studied cases of this are the occurrences during the shock of an accident, grave illness, or surgery. The people usually become aware of themselves floating free of the situation's trauma and looking down at their own bodies with a sense of surprise and relief. Various other adventures follow, as we shortly will see. The other commonly reported form of this happens during sleep, when the body is left behind during visits to distant places or persons, or to the astral planes. These differ from ordinary dreams because the experience is, subjectively, far more vivid and *real*.

— "Spontaneous" healing and recovery from body illnesses when conventional medical treatments have failed. These are some of the most convincing documentations of the fact that there is more to life than flesh.

— Group highs, as in a religious ceremony, a live music concert, or a sports rally. This can most easily be noted in the difference between listening to a record and attending a good live performance — the difference is hard to describe, but easy to sense.

— Being alive. This is the most universal, but probably the most overlooked, spiritual phenomenon of them all. Most of us do have the awareness of feeling more alive or less alive at different times. Also, if someone really wants to live, they can survive almost anything, but if they want out of the physical plane, any stray infection can kill the body. There is solid evidence, as described, for example, in Richard Gerber's *Vibrational Medicine*, for the fact that without an energizing spirit the human body is nothing more than a comatose vegetable.

There are other kinds of psychic phenomena and many variations of those noted above, but these are some of the major ones frequently reported. Sometimes, there are other possible explanations when a single incident from this catalogue happens. But there is a principle called the Multiplication Rule of Probability at work here. Stated oversimply, it is that the probability of all of a series of events occurring is the multiplied product of each one occurring. Thus, if there is a fifty-percent chance that a single psychic experience was the result of coincidence, the probability that twenty of them resulted from coincidence alone is less than one in one million. *Tens of thousands* of cases which now exist on file cannot, therefore, be explained away. And for some, such as the documented child prodigies, there is no plausible physical-plane explanation, even if we conjure up the wildest set of coincidences.

Many people who have had direct psychic experiences and awareness of psychic influences have remarked to me about their on-again, off-again, come-and-go nature. Why are they sometimes conscious of them, sometimes not?

From the data of our emerging paranormal picture, the answer to this question seems simple. Both psychic abilities and levels of consciousness are matters of the spirit. An ordinary human being's spiritual awareness and connectedness waxes and wanes under various circumstances, evidently even including dominant brain-wave pattern at any given time. As spiritual consciousness fluctuates, so does one's awareness of psychic influences. But this is only the beginning of our story of supernormal experiences.

4

Profound Paranormal Experiences

Several years ago, while conducting a seminar on youth culture at a major west coast university, I met a young man who was hosting the event. He was the president of the Student Association and evidently the brightest, most promising, graduate student in his department. He had already published some papers and had just won a prestigious fellowship. He was the epitome of a brilliant student on his way to Big Things professionally.

A couple of years later, while idly chatting with a colleague from that university, I casually asked about him. The colleague got a puzzled look and said, well, that was a funny story. The young man had begun writing some very strange papers and then one day had just walked off from his fellowship. He then took up with a girl who was into the Whole Earth movement and they had wandered around the Pacific islands for awhile. Then they had come back and moved to Arizona, where he was doing some kind of body-healing work and spending a lot of time with the Indians. I asked how all this had come about and the colleague shrugged and said, *something* must have happened to him! Something, indeed. With the help of our emerging picture, we can now guess what that something might have been.

Most of the spiritually based experiences we looked at in the last two chapters, although they are universal, are only a sort of background to daily living on the physical plane. They are usually peripheral and subliminal and they can easily be ignored or explained away in a doubting social climate. The participants themselves often remain somewhat unconvinced.

There is, however, another range of experiences in which the experiencer is fully conscious, if not superconscious, of what happened, and in which the person is utterly convinced of their paranormal nature, even in the face of a legion of disbelievers. Because of their intensity and their transforming aftereffects, such experiences can only be called *profound*.

These profound paranormal experiences have four main features in common.

One: In their raw intensity and vividness, they are preternaturally *real* to the experiencer, far above and beyond the realness of ordinary events. This overwhelming sense of realness is so strong that it does not fade with the passing of years or even decades.

Two: The person emerges from the experience with the unshakable conviction that he or she is most fundamentally and essentially an immortal spiritual being. Along with this realization, the fear of death greatly diminishes or evaporates.

Three: The aftereffects of the experience prove to be life-transforming. This transformation can be swift or a slow unfolding, but it is always significant, and it is noticeable to the individual and to others.

Four: As part of this transformation, there is a significant shift and shakeup in the experiencer's priorities, purposes, games, and goals. For that person, *things are never the same again*.

What sorts of events can produce such impressive impacts and changes? The most extensively researched and documented cases are those involving near-death experiences (NDEs) of people who have almost died or been pronounced clinically dead as a result of major accidents, illnesses or surgery. But there are many other types of extraordinary experiences that have produced similar results. A sudden vivid, conscious connection with a spirit guide; a cosmic awakening resulting from a program of meditation or physical yoga practices; an "ah-ha!" realization while pursuing some spiritual tradition such as Kabbalah or Wicca; visiting some Holy Ground; a conscious out-of-the-body experience; an overwhelming sense of *deja vu* while visiting some historical location. The list is almost endless.

Such experiences often occur spontaneously, without any sort of forewarning. In his book, *Lifetimes*, Frederick Lenz reports tracing down many cases of totally spontaneous remembrances of past lives which profoundly influenced the individuals involved. It seems that any incident which leads to a strong awareness of one's essential spiritual nature can produce these kinds of far reaching results.

It must be emphasized that, according to the reports, these experiences are many times more intense and moving than such ordinary peak experiences as romantic love or the temporary collective high of a beautiful religious service or a live rock concert. This is probably another example of that familiar observation, "If you've experienced it, you know; if you haven't, you can't really know." However, you don't have to have had one of these experiences in order to gain some understanding of their nature and impact.

How widespread are such experiences? We don't really know, but the numbers now appear to be much larger than anyone previously thought. Here are some conservative projections, based upon recent National Opinion Research Center and Gallup Poll data, and on my own speculations from culling the literature. Note well — these are only ballpark estimates, but they are startling. There are evidently more than ten million people in the world who have had strong near-death experiences in which they remember leaving their bodies and seeing them as if from outside, visiting the Beyond, meeting disembodied beings and bathing in a loving light, then returning to finish out their current life tasks. There are several hundred thousand people in this country alone who clearly and consciously remember some material from previous lives and are utterly convinced of its validity. There are at least five million Americans who are convinced that they have directly communicated with disembodied spirits. Some hundreds of thousands of our countrymen have a conscious awareness of having been outside of their physical bodies. There are tens upon tens of thousands of people in America today who have experienced some major form of miracle healing, a fair number of whom are alive today despite the dire diagnoses of conventional medical professionals. There are at least two million people in this country who, through pursuing some form of self-realization, have achieved a significantly higher state of consciousness. And Ingo Swann estimates that some ten percent of the population has had significant ESP experiences. So we are surely not talking about just a few fringe group members here. This adds up to a lot of people, and many more are reporting such experiences as time passes. All these people are still very much a minority — but a growing one.

The vast majority of these people don't advertise. In fact, researchers have found that, at least until recently, the majority remain quiet about their experiences, telling only a few intimates or someone they have found who seems to understand. Some, after a vain attempt or two, tell no one. This is one main reason why past investigations grossly underestimated the prevalence of these phenomena. Quiet or not, however, the experiencers do pursue a significantly changed lifestyle.

We know that extreme circumstances will sometimes bring about strong paranormal experiences. But many people under extreme conditions don't report such happenings. Are there social or psychological factors that predispose people to having such profound experiences? Not that we know of at this time. Psychologist and researcher, Kenneth Ring, for instance, found no significant difference in rates between men and women, or between the previously religious and nonreligious. If these experiences play favorites, it is along lines that have not yet been discovered. It seems that they can happen to anyone and are potentially available to everyone.

Some of the people who have had such transforming experiences would seem on the surface to be unlikely candidates. By their own testimony, many were previously self-seeking, materialistically oriented, and quite uncaring about others. The majority were not "seekers" nor had they been much interested in things spiritual prior to their experience. Some felt they were chosen to have the experience by Higher Forces as a means of "waking them up." Some felt it was a chance offered them to "mend their ways," to turn back from a downhill slide they'd been on. Others felt it was a matter of circumstance and that it could befall any human being under the proper set of conditions. Their understanding is that the cosmos or All That Is is set up this way.

Whether there are earthly predisposing factors and whatever they might be, it is certainly true that anyone can seek and sometimes find such transcending experiences through a host of widely available awareness-expansion regimens such as meditation, yoga, Monroe's brain hemispheric synchronization, and so on. There is an old Eastern saying that there are many paths to the top of the mountain.

There would seem to be two broad sorts of profound paranormal experiences: those that happen suddenly and spontaneously, like the near-death experiences, and those resulting from a sometimes lengthy and arduous practice of a consciousness-expanding discipline. However, even though the entry points are various and many, the raw experiences themselves are remarkably similar, whatever brought them about. Near-death researchers such as Ring and Moody, the Tibetan monks, and a good many others have demonstrated that, however one gets there, one gets to a similar place.

What "place" is it that they get to? By all accounts, it seems to be a rather fantastic inner place involving a fundamental shift of perspectives. Before the event the person may or may not have believed in spirituality, but if they did it was only a rather incidental part of their lives, like the sociable Sunday churchgoer. But this raw experience brought home a stark, immediate awareness that they are spirits above and beyond their bodies and that the cosmos is alive. Believing, if it had existed, was transformed into *knowing*. Faith became *fact* for them. The experience itself usually initiated a massive reshuffling of priorities. What had been important became unimportant. And spirituality or compassion, if they had been unimportant or taken for granted before, now became vitally important to the person. These shifts were always in the direction of less concern about status and material things and more concern with humanitarian values and spiritual growth. After such profound paranormal experiences, *the person literally is never the same again*.

To put the point another way, profound spiritual experiences have an overriding power. It seems that our spiritual sensitivities are ordinarily so dulled and distracted that only the strongest psychic experiences can fully reach our consciousness. They must be intense enough to overcome all our psychological barriers and disbeliefs and our dominant focus on the continuous stream of physical-plane happenings. When this happens, the person is blown free of all the clutter and literally experiences an enlightenment. As sociologist Charles Flynn's research respondents asserted, one never "gets over" the resulting experience.

Ring, Kubler-Ross, Flynn, and other paranormal researchers found, among those they worked with, that the profound experience itself was not the end but only the beginning of an unfolding process, a "seed incident." The new perspectives inevitably produced subsequent adjustments in the person's thinking, feelings, behavior, and relationships with others. From all accounts, such adjustments do not cease at some point, but continue to unfold from there on out. In other words, the profound experience launches the person upon a spiritual odyssey.

The post-experience event of trying to share the experience is often painful and frustrating. When the person attempts to tell others about this enthralling experience, he or she is typically told it was nothing but a hallucination and is often then admonished that it's best to keep quiet about it. In near-death experiences, for instance, even spouses and close family members tend to dismiss the incident as a trauma-induced psychosis that the person will "get over" when she or he "recovers." Even after all the recent national NDE publicity, most hospital staff are still disbelieving and disapproving. In the NDE literature are cases in which hospital personnel have warned patients to keep quiet about such things or they might be sent to the psychiatric wards — a threat indeed for anyone who knows anything about psychiatric wards. Needless to say, such responses do not promote open communication or full disclosure. Outside hospital settings, individuals have encountered similar kinds of derisive rejection upon telling others the details of a past-life connection. The fact is that these kinds of profound experiences lie beyond our conventional mainstream society's views of the world. They usually are joked about, explained away, and condemned. But they keep happening in ever-increasing numbers, partly because of advances in emergency medical technology. And they surely cannot be explained away to those who have directly experienced them.

We cannot altogether blame those who become derisive after hearing such tales, because they seem so *fantastic*. And when they occur spontaneously, as in an NDE, they may be totally out of character with the person's previous personality and outlook. A farmer telling his wife and his country doctor about being out of his body, visiting realms of light, and communicating with angelic spirits is almost bound to cause a stir and some concern for the man's stability. The profound experiencer's frustrations are compounded by the fact that the experience, all respondents agree, is fundamentally *indescribable* in any human terms. So we have a sticky interpersonal situation: an awe-struck person haltingly trying to tell dumbfounded listeners about an uncanny experience. It's no wonder that all parties involved usually become vexed.

These communication difficulties notwithstanding, the person cannot go back to the way things were before. The experience, along with its accompanying insights and convictions, must somehow be integrated into daily life in that person's previously established world. The contrasts between the spiritual and physical realms are no longer just vague ideas; they are now stark, immediate situations that have to be dealt with in some way. One woman reported extreme difficulty reconciling new, vaulting perspectives and wisdom gained during an NDE with her family's traditional role expectations of her as a midwestern wife and mother. Another woman, who had successfully carried out the miracle healing of a grave illness one weekend, had a very difficult time "coming down" and functioning as a routine office worker the next day.

For many individuals, a fully and vividly remembered NDE or other profound psychic experience is perhaps the ultimate in culture shock. Imagine that you, an ordinary human minding your own mundane business, are suddenly propelled into an awesomely different set of conditions and bathed in uncanny sensations and perceptions. These sensations and perceptions are probably overwhelming and utterly unexpected. And maybe you encounter a "dead" comrade or loved one who greets and joyously enfolds you. You may be overcome with the realization that you are experiencing the *reality* that lies behind the veils of earthly illusions. This might be coupled with the discovery that *you* are alive and conscious, independent of any physical body.

Such an incident is, to say the least, a startling departure from the ordinary stream of experiences. There is some evidence that many people who have such experiences during accidents or surgery find them so hard to accept that they blank them out afterwards. In such cases, the left brain seems to deny the possibility of such experiences in the first place, and then erases the experience from the conscious mind when it does occur.

Those who retain conscious memories of such profound experiences often discover, almost accidentally, how great an effect they have had on them. They often find, to their surprise, that they are now less irritable with other people, that they are much more accepting about things that previously upset or bothered them, that the "same" world seems brighter than before. Also, they find themselves tending to adjust and reconcile any spiritual and mundane discrepancies by drifting toward more alignment with their newfound spiritual viewpoints and desires. This is not so much a deliberate program as an unfolding that carries them along.

Such a drifting may well include some interpersonal turmoil, an eventual major career change, or a divorce. But one thing is clear: the life-changing effects of the profound experience roll on and on.

You don't have to be a "good" person to have a profound spiritual experience or to be transformed and uplifted as a result of it. These profound spiritual experiences sometimes befall persons whom society regards as ne'er-do-wells, and the resulting life changes are, if anything, even more dramatic. The "before" and "after" shift can be very impressive, a total turnaround of attitudes and behavior. The person may simply walk away from drugs, alcohol, promiscuity, or a wastrel lifestyle. Not infrequently, such persons then are drawn to work involving the caregiving and attempted rescues of their former party companions. Numbers are impossible to estimate, but you often see these people entering careers in social work, nursing, special program teaching, even the ministry. In addition to their increased compassion, they have the advantage of really knowing what they're talking about.

There are internal, interpersonal, and societal effects of profound paranormal experiences. The internal effects can include a reshuffling of what is important and unimportant, a growth in compassion and understanding of others, some frustration about the way the world is, a shift toward spiritual interests and concerns, a loss of fear of death, and a strengthened sense of self as an integral part of a living cosmic whole. All of these add up to what a great many experiencers from many paths describe as an *awakening.* As one woman described it to me, "It was just like I had been sleepwalking before . . . . I was asleep inside and didn't even know it. Looking back, I don't think I was a very nice person."

Among all the inner changes, the overwhelming realization that one is a deathless and immortal spirit seems to be the hottest single item, beside which everything else pales to insignificance. Many people *believe* in some form of immortality; profound experience veterans *know* it.

What does a person do with such a realization? A few say they tried to ignore it in order to cope with a disbelieving society, but they found this was impossible to do. Some threw themselves into religion, but often found the organized churches to be petty and dogmatic and sectarian, compared with the transcendental realities they had directly experienced. Some others began broadcasting their new viewpoints to as many other people as possible, despite any opposition. Most became "better persons" by virtually anyone's standards.

"Better person" translates into interpersonal behavior that is more pleasant and helpful to other people. One woman said that after her husband's NDE during major surgery he began to display a lot more of all the things she'd always liked about him and far fewer of those that had caused chronic upsets between them. She remarked that *maybe the whole world needed to have a near-death experience.*

I have known a good many people (including myself sometimes) who have engaged in much hand wringing about the conditions of the world, yet have remained quite self-centered and ungiving in their own interpersonal lives. Not so the profound spiritual experience veterans.

The vast majority of veterans don't put on robes and sandals, but they do change their ways, according to the reports of those who knew them both before and after. The profound experience evidently provides a spiritual "boost" sufficient to blow off their previously established interpersonal habits and to provide perspectives for developing new ones. To put it simply, they become more empathic, compassionate, and caregiving toward others, whether family, acquaintances, or strangers. This change is not some intellectual decision, not a matter of the head like a New Year's resolution, but an awakening of the heart and soul.

The interpersonal behavior of profound experience veterans typically manifests a marked decrease in negatives and a marked increase in positives. They back off from or sidestep competiveness, if their winning entails others losing; they get upset and irritated with others much less often; they develop a generic distaste for violence;

they stop being constantly judgmental about others; they are not good gossipers. Most of them certainly don't become saints, but they are not likely to be thorns in other people's sides.

On the positive side they *help* other people, without counting the cost or looking for immediate rewards in return. They don't measure others by how useful they can be to them. From their own statements, this openness and helpfulness is not a matter of duty but of pleasure. In fact it seems often to become the major source of pleasure in their lives.

To a lot of people, all this may sound sweetie-pie and goodie-two-shoes and just too good for the realities of this world. I've discussed this with people who felt such behavior was fine but "unrealistic." I've talked with others who almost sneered at this kind of lifestyle. After hearing about the changes in one NDE experiencer, a sophomore coed giggled and said, "Doesn't seem like much of a party animal." A man in his early forties, who had had an unhappy cult involvement, told me he read everything he could find on the occult and spiritual, but sometimes he felt like going to a dirty movie with lots of sex and violence just for a break.

I have pondered these kinds of responses and sought to understand them. *Why would some people belittle qualities, when they are actually manifested, that are usually considered some of the best aspects of humanity?* The accumulated research indicates that most of those directly involved with the profound experience veterans are happy about the changes in them, whatever they think of their stories. For instance, Kenneth Ring's *Heading Toward Omega* cites many such cases. I think many who have only indirectly heard about these cases find the gulf between such ideas of spirituality and their own more "down-to-earth" perspectives too great to easily bridge. This gulf is then psychologically handled by rejecting the paranormal worldview. Most of those who had doubting and derisive responses to the profound stories seemed to be deeply immersed and introverted into physical-plane situations and games. *To open themselves up to a transcendental spiritual perspective would almost inevitably call for a reassessment of all their beliefs and life routines*—a formidable task for anyone. Easier just to dismiss the "outlandish" views and turn away.

But a good many of those who hear about such unusual experiences don't turn away. Many people find a rescue from their own uncertainties, dissatisfactions, and fears in the accounts of those who have found a spiritual awakening. They provide comfort and hope and a more vaulting vision, a welcome alternative to the mainstream culture's fare. The books published on these profound experiences keep rolling through printing after printing, so they are obviously providing *something* for many people. A home improvement contractor told me he read a few pages of such books every night and that it kept him alive.

Nowhere is the difference between direct spiritual experience and organized church dogma more apparent than in the new religious attitudes of profound experience veterans. By and large, they say their religious views and feelings are now transcendental and universalistic. They see the same vaulting messages underlying all organized religions, and they lose all interest in divisive doctrinal disputes. As a result, some doctrinaire religionists find them blasphemous and threatening and have even condemned them as dupes of Satan. Meanwhile, they go about the world attempting to share the Light they say they have directly experienced. They report that their heightened sensitivity to the spiritual essence of others as well as themselves is accompanied by a growth in interpersonal empathy and an increasing experience of psychic phenomena of all kinds. Because of this they simply *can't* ignore the feelings of others any more.

What are the societal-level impacts of people with such profound experiences? This is something of a "who knows" guessing game that we'll look at in later chapters, but a couple of points can be made now. There is a well-known phenomenon called "the ripple effect." The experience veterans touch the lives of those around them, who in turn touch the lives of others, who then touch others . . . and so on. I recently traced one such strand through six links and no doubt there were other strands emanating from the NDE person, a Kansas grandmother. With enough such ripples occurring, the cumulative results could be a wave.

The other point is that through public lectures, television appearances, and books, veterans of these experiences have been providing some provocative alternative perspectives on death, the meaning of human life, relationships, and the nature of the cosmos. What influences these alternative viewpoints will eventually have on our society is still a wide-open question. But we do know that some people's lives have been eased and enriched as a result. For the rest, we'll see. At least we get to live in interesting times.

Several factors are presently at work to greatly increase the number of people having profound spiritual experiences. New medical techniques are reviving people who would have simply died in earlier times. Information about new spiritual techniques that can produce paranormal effects are being widely diffused throughout the world. Belief that they are possible and valid is growing. As these trends continue, we may have nothing less than an eventual groundswell of awakenings.

There are, then, a growing number of people "loose in the world" who have had a profound spiritual awakening as a result of some profound mystical experience. But there is another important group, an even larger number of people, who have had a *partial* spiritual awakening. They're an interesting lot, because they have one foot in each realm and attempt to straddle some sort of middle ground. And they are everywhere. Odds are that this author and many of his readers are among them. And they probably make up the large majority of the people actively involved in the spiritual awakening movement.

One might say that these partially awakened people have been *stirred* but not fully transformed. Any set of conditions capable of producing a profound experience will sometimes produce only a partial one. But a very long list of other things have triggered such spiritual stirrings: a book, hearing a charismatic speaker, the Alcoholics

Anonymous program, a psychedelic drug experience, exposure to a fringe spiritual cult, a trip to a wilderness area, the shakeup resulting from a life crisis, or just some spontaneous welling up inside. It seems that virtually *anything* can serve to remind people that they are more than flesh. Such triggering incidents are what Marilyn Ferguson calls "entry points," the first stage of a personal crossover into the New Age.

The thing that is unique about such individuals, in their present stage of development, is their ambivalence. The profound experience veterans have unequivocally moved over to the side of spirituality, while the partially awakened manifest as hybrids.

Once upon a time I thought many of the latter were just fooling around with the supernatural, but since then I've learned how wrong I was. On investigation, their appearance of dilettantism often turns out to be a camouflage, a means of "passing" in conventional society, the inner tensions concealed to avoid risking their closest relationships. I know a middle-aged woman, a bookkeeper, who deliberately cultivates the notion among her family and friends that she is just an eccentric, in order to be left in peace to pursue her spiritual interests. The felt need for such camouflage is diminishing now in our transition times, but some of it will no doubt persist until there is a full-blown world transformation.

Over the years, through interviewing, counselling, and in other capacities, I have made the acquaintance of several hundred such partially awakened people. As one might suppose, their present lives seem to fall somewhere between those of profound experience veterans and ordinary members of society.

Are they "better off" than the ordinary person? There has been very little systematic study of them, and also "better off" is mostly a matter of personal viewpoint, but some observations can be made. I can't offer any percentage figures, but I have seen many of these people straighten out their lives to some extent after the stirring. For instance, I have seen a good many of them just walk away from drugs and an aimless lifestyle. I also have seen some of them establish stable intimate relationships for the first time in their lives.

The partially awakened certainly do not become a legion of saints. You still might not get the best business deal from them and they still might run off with your spouse. At the present stage of their journey, they tend to be consumers as much as producers of spiritual phenomena. But you can perceive a significant gentling and mellowing in the way they conduct their lives. They do change. They move away from the more competitive, violent, and exploitative forms of human behavior, and there is a noticeable movement toward more considerate and cooperative styles. They also become seekers to a greater or lesser degree, looking beyond the mainstream social patterns and questing after alternatives.

Their seekings are frequently an on-again, off-again thing because they still are wrapped up in some major physical-plane goal, such as getting through school, or raising two toddlers, or getting established in a career. They feel that they're simply not in a position to drop everything and singlemindedly pursue spiritual development. Also, they may be immersed in working through their earthly habits, attachments, and addictions. For these and other reasons, they may not be ready yet for a full awakening. In their personal accounts, Robert Monroe, Jane Roberts (the channel for Seth), Shirley MacLaine, and many other New Age notables, describe a long developmental unfolding from early stirrings to later transformations that stretched over years or even decades.

The fact that the partially awakened have a double perspective on life seems to be both an enrichment and a source of trouble for them. The trouble arises from attempting to reconcile and integrate the two perspectives, but this tension also provides an impetus to propel them forward in their search and journey. When they are in a spiritual mode, mundane affairs can seem petty and unimportant, and they may wonder how they got caught up in so much resentment and fear. But when they are "down," operating "rationally" in the workaday world, it may be hard for them to recollect spiritual moments, and a curtain of doubt about their authenticity may fall. The partially awakened person may appear to see-saw back and forth between these two perspectives for some major portion of their lives. But a close examination will almost always show that real growth is occurring. Sometimes this progress is hard to see in the short run, but from a larger perspective it becomes clear. Seth, Emmanuel, Michael, and other discarnate teachers have pointed out that one eventually understands that *no lifetime is ever wasted.*

Partially awakened people are probably the major customers for spiritual books and practitioners of self-development regimens. Many of them shop around, not necessarily in a dilettantish way, as part of their questing. This questing may seem restless because of the integration they are striving to achieve. There are now millions upon millions of such people, and if profound experience veterans are the "stars" of the current spiritual movement, these people are its backbone.

Scientific research is now amassing empirical evidence that many of the regimens practiced by the partially awakened are in themselves healthful. It has been established, for instance, that meditation helps reduce blood pressure levels and handle stress. Physical (Hatha) yoga has been shown to help alleviate many ills and to help restore flexibility and vigor even among the elderly. Various "mind machines," such as the Monroe Institute's brain hemispheric synchronization program, have shown the promise of increasing all-around mental abilities. And participation in Alcoholics Anonymous is certainly healthier than alcoholism. (For summaries of some of this research, see Michael Hutchinson's *Megabrain.*)

How easy would it be to deliberately produce transformations in ordinary people similar to those occurring among profound experience veterans? Sociologist Dr. Charles Flynn addressed this question in a series of fascinating experiments. Flynn conducted "Love Projects" in his university classes, first showing students videotapes of NDE interviews and having them read Leo Buscaglia's book, *Love.* He then had them go out and relate to someone they probably would never have related to, under ordinary circumstances, such as an elderly shut-in or an unpopular dorm-mate. The results were very exciting. As a result of these contacts, highly significant attitude shifts toward qualities usually considered spiritual occurred among the overwhelming majority of the students. The lives of those they had connected with also were enriched. A follow-up questionnaire a year later showed that these results had persisted. The project experience had, in fact, changed the direction of many of these students' lives. Some had switched majors to one of the caregiving professions; others went on befriending people they would previously have hardly even noticed. Individual changes thus were continuing to spread outward into the larger society.

So there are things going on in the world besides the latest media news briefs.

5

Disembodied Spirits

Several years ago someone said to me, "I've got to be at work in a few minutes, but tell me about disembodied spirits." At his question, all the reports I had read and all of the direct experiences I had had, and all the Western and Eastern writings I'd gone through swirled before me. I believe I shrugged helplessly and said I'd talk with him later. As he was hurrying off, I did say, "Well, you've been one before and you'll be one again." As he was rushing off to handle some client's accounts, he said, "Yes, that's why I want to know."

Since that time the swirl has resolved into a more coherent picture that is part of the larger emerging spiritual story. This more coherent picture is the result of some courageous questing and hard work on the part of a lot of people—and a little help from their discarnate friends.

The following pages are a collage culled from the works of a long list of dedicated paranormal investigators including Harold Sherman, Helen Wambach, Edgar Cayce, Joel Whitton, Robert Monroe and his Explorer Teams, Iris Belhayes, and Gavin and Yvonne Frost, to name a few. The channeled communications of Michael, Seth, Emmanuel, Enid, and Orin were also drawn upon. Some of the interpretations also stem from my personal experiences in psychic counselling, exorcising discarnates, and astral contacts.

Perhaps no subject has been as riddled with legend and superstition and dogma as that of disembodied spirits. *A disembodied spirit, to put it simply, is a being not presently inhabiting a physical body*. The idea that one has to inhabit a body to be alive would evidently cause vast humor throughout the cosmos. We are all spiritual beings; we humans just happen to be presently dwelling in homo sapiens biological units and inhabiting the physical plane. To be in-human, as Robert Monroe calls it, is a very temporary and special circumstance that is one "short" phase in our spiritual evolution. So to call spirits "them" is very misleading. Modern scientific theories and studies are discovering that reality is multidimensional. It would appear that disembodied spirits exist within other dimensions which interface with the physical plane.

The true nature of spirits far exceeds most human conjectures and stereotypes about them. Most traditional religions and mainstream societies have sharply divided all discarnate spirits into two opposing camps—good and evil—with a third residual category of lost souls. Evidently, this notion couldn't be further from the truth. In the actual Beyond, among spirits themselves, such a good-bad distinction doesn't seem to exist. *The* true distinction, and the most important one, is degree of spiritual evolvement. There are only less and more evolved beings. Less evolved beings can be troublesome, whether they have bodies or not, but this is "only" the working out of the evolutionary process.

In our ghost stories, horror fiction, and religious preachments, humans have grossly maligned disembodied spirits. But the overwhelming majority of reported actual spirit contacts throughout the world have, in fact, been beneficent. This conclusion is further supported by the overwhelming majority of reports from those who themselves temporarily became disembodied spirits during near-death-experiences. They met Beings of Light who overwhelmed them with compassion and understanding. Some disembodied spirits are very highly evolved, but many seem to be "just plain folks" who happen to be living somewhere else.

Discarnate spirits vary in character to a far greater extent than embodied humans do. There is a much wider range in the Beyond than here on Earth. As with humans, each spirit has a unique "signature" or pattern of energy. This is how they recognize one another, and how we recognize past-life companions. As with humans, however, there are also certain types or categories among them. There are blithe spirits, troubled spirits, mean spirits, wise spirits, playful spirits, kindred spirits, earthbound spirits, pretentious spirits, and so on. There are spirits of transcendental, loving wisdom and there are dumb spirits.

It should be emphasized again that spirits can no more be neatly divided into categories of good or bad than humans can. Every spirit has its own character, complete with character peculiarities. So a spirit can be loving, but narrow-minded and contemptuous of other viewpoints; it can be indifferent toward adults, but kindly and protective toward children; it can have delusions of grandeur and be touchy about certain subjects; it can have a panoramic "outsider" view of history and current events, but no in-depth knowledge of economics; it can be stupified and in a daze; it can be so highly evolved that its images and messages are almost impossible for in-humans to comprehend. There are also spirits who were animals when last embodied. The "ghost" of a household pet will sometimes hang around for awhile.

Spirits often continue to manifest echoes and "after-images" from their recent earthly programming, although usually in diluted and somewhat transcendent forms. They can be stuck in some earthly circumstance because of their own considerations and obsessions, but they will usually snap out of it and move on after a time. Or higher level beings will help to nudge them out. There is great, helpful cooperation among spirits, the more evolved assisting the less evolved. But the less evolved must be ready and willing to *receive* this assistance. Free choice remains a basic principle of experience at all evolvement levels, as a necessary facet of independent personal growth.

Aside from unique, individual character, the most distinguishing difference among spirits is their level of spiritual evolvement. This includes the abilities they possess and the uses to which they put them. Accounts from individuals who have had conscious contact with spirits differ as to the number of levels of spiritual development and the realms they typically inhabit, but there is widespread consensus on the gross divisions. The diversity of opinion seems to come from the fact that all of our data is reported by those presently in a human condition, with its inherent perceptual limitations. I have the strong feeling that in this endeavor we are like a group of children trying to describe the grownup world.

There is quite a range among less evolved beings, running from very low-level spirits, to "earthbound spirits," to those who have recently died and are in their between-lives period before rebirth. Very low-level beings abide in a coarse astral wavelength, a shadowy place of dazed and aimless wanderings. These beings may be in a somewhat unpleasant dream state of their own making. They may strongly desire to have a human body in order to join in the game, but find it difficult to penetrate into the earth plane because of their own limitations and beliefs. They resonate with the grosser emotions—resentment, anger, fear, lust. They are no real threat to most humans, who can easily banish them. But it is not advisable to play around with them. They are not really dangerous but they can create discomfort and they get off on fear and other intense low-level emotions. They resonate with some incarnate humans on a Like Attracts Like basis. If you are bothered by them, just tell them to go away, or to go to the Light. Or call upon a higher being to handle them, which they can easily do. With a bit of training you can often handle and free them yourself. Iris Belhayes book, *Spirit Guides*, shows you how to do this. But don't ask them to stay for supper.

Earthbound spirits usually have more awareness than these lowest level ones. But, for one reason or another, they are not yet willing to let go of their compulsive immersions in the physical plane. The being may be obsessively attached to loved ones, such as a spouse or children, or to some personal unfinished enterprise, such as the building of a house or a company they had started. They may be compulsively clinging to some locale where they felt safe and secure. They may even be refusing to recognize the fact that they have separated from their physical body. For whatever reason, they have failed as yet to go on to a normal astral phase of development. It is no accident that funeral rites around the world have involved rituals for releasing the spirit of the newly deceased, helping it to go onward in its journey.

These spirits are the source of the legends about troubled souls who can find no peace until some earthly situation is resolved, such as bringing their murderer to justice or saving their child from some difficult situation. They will sometimes communicate in dreams, when the barriers to receptivity are down, with those humans they have ties with. Note that they comprise only a small portion of all disembodied spirits. Note also that they are upset, frustrated, or obsessed, but not evil.

Earthbound spirits "hang around," and so we have haunted buildings, woods, and hills. These hauntings can be pleasant or unpleasant to humans, broadcasting warm, nice feelings or shivery, spooky feelings. Many cultures have perceived that such spirits are virtually everywhere, peopling the entire environment with invisible presences. They knew that their environment was *alive*. In our own time, such perceptions of the aliveness of nature have been largely lost, although they are currently being rediscovered by many people. In her provocative book, *Agartha*, Meredith Lady Young describes her own unfolding awareness of just how spiritually alive the world around her is.

From the now innumerable reports of visitations, it seems that the newly dead often spend a bit of time in an earthbound state, lingering over some physical plane connection, or trying to communicate some last messages to those still incarnate. But the links are two-way. Intense and prolonged grieving on the part of incarnates can "bind" the departed spirits and keep them earthbound for longer than need be. The most common theme in their last messages is that the departed person is doing fine (if not better than ever) and to let go of them for now—they'll see you later. So we often have the "dead" comforting the "living." *What an egocentric viewpoint it is to consider only in-humans "alive".*

Above the earthbound level are the majority of the recently deceased and those involved in their between-lives sojourn. These experience the astral planes as joyous, filled with warmth and wonder, and truly paranormal experiences and realizations. There are unearthly beauties to intensely experience and enthralling reunions with old companions and loved ones. There are luminous landscapes and endless things to do, and even "schools" where one can learn the "real story." Previous earthly lives are evaluated and the lessons drawn from them. Plans for future development are made in concert with old companions and more evolved spirits. Also, one can just goof off for awhile on a vacation from the heavier vibration levels. For those who have just come through an especially heavy or traumatic physical lifetime, it is a period of rest and recuperation.

These beings can sometimes be communicated with by humans who have a strong focus or intention and they can be called upon by sensitive mediums. But the large gap in vibration frequencies makes communication difficult. Also, these spirits tend to be occupied with their own affairs.

The more highly evolved spirits have had more of an awakening and often act as guides, counsellors, and sometimes rescuers of less evolved beings. They often greet and help orient new arrivals from the physical plane. They help provide intuitions and inspirations for those on the physical plane who ask and care to listen. They seem to be sort of cosmic second-graders helping the younger children across the street and watching out for them a bit. They may have completed or nearly completed their own reincarnation cycles, although they are really just beginning their spiritual evolvement on the astral levels. They are not all-wise or free of biases, but they are universally described as compassionate, loving, and understanding—a real pleasure to meet. They also seem to have an irrepressible sense of humor.

Above these are spirits involved in the more panoramic activities of the cosmos, which seem to be largely incomprehensible to those still incarnate on the physical plane. These activities seem to include the development, maintenance, and enhancement of various dimensional realities within the All That Is. They are evidently involved in consciousness-expansion work on many different levels. And they are available as advisors to the less evolved. They probably include the Beings of Light (sometimes encountered by NDEs) and the high-order spirits, such as Seth, Michael, Orin, and Mentor, channelled by spiritually awakened humans. Evidently only a small portion of their full beingness is manifested in such earth-plane contacts.

Above these are even more transcendent beings: the Christs and Buddhas and their fellows who walk many planes and aid in spiritual growth wherever they go.

And above all these is *something* which may encompass everything, that leaves all descriptive words and symbols far, far behind. Since it is essentially nameless, any name will do.

Evidently, consciousness-expansion is an endless open-ended game with no upper limits. And it is an unthinkably vast cooperative endeavor.

The nature and abilities of spirits obviously depend greatly on their current level of evolvement. But they all seem to share certain capabilities that are inherent in their essential nature. Spirits can sense and use a wide range of vibrational wavelengths. They can directly share thoughts and emotions. They can "read" pasts and the threads of various probable futures. They can move through space by intention, but they evidently cannot penetrate the higher astral realms until they are sufficiently evolved to manifest the necessary finer wavelengths.

Beings love experience, and they enjoy drawing the lessons of knowledge and understanding from it. Their attitude seems to be like that of a gourmet who loves to sample different wines and dishes.

Disembodied spirits have less tunnel vision and a more panoramic grasp of situations and scenes than the spirits currently incarnated as humans. Their degree of wisdom depends on their evolvement level. Whatever the level, they vary in individual characteristics, abilities, and style. Some are artists, some are healers and guides, some are explorers, some are sages, and so on. Those on the higher level can do a lot of conscious choosing, while lower level ones operate more on compulsions and tropisms, like the automatic tropism of a plant turning its foliage toward the sun. In sum, disembodied spirits vary even more than humans do.

Spirits don't know everything—they are not omniscient. Their knowledge and wisdom varies by level and by individual character. There are dumb spirits.

Spirits don't always agree, because each has its own perspectives and its own limits of awareness. But they are not very quarrelsome and seem to operate mostly on a "live and let live" basis. Contentiousness seems to disappear as they become more evolved. What can you do to a deathless being anyway?

One common question is: Where do all the spirits come from to inhabit the growing number of bodies produced by our current population explosion? The answer is simple. There are many, many more spirits than human incarnates, so there is no shortage whatsoever.

To what extent can discarnate spirits affect the embodied? Obviously such spirits don't have physical hands but they are very capable of creating what people in the sixties called "vibes"—mental-emotional energy vibrations. These can be sensed in some dim, subliminal way by most people and they can sometimes act as mood influencers and subtle mind influencers. The intensity of such impingements varies tremendously from negligible to almost overwhelming. The range of sensations and emotions that can be picked up also varies tremendously, from red rage and stark fright to uneasiness, from sexual excitement to loving, enfolding warmth, unconditional acceptance, and cosmic joyfulness. Most reports indicate that the overwhelming majority of such ghostly impingements are benign. Also, humans can choose what impingements, if any, they let in.

A great deal of the contact with spirits occurs during sleep and other off-line states, such as drowsiness and daydreaming. In such states, the incarnate person's focus broadens out from the physical plane to make such interchanges possible. Such "sleep work" experiences are just as valid and growth-enhancing as waking experiences, according to Seth, Michael, and other high spirits.

From their side of the veil, discarnate spirits, especially earthbound ones, are evidently often frustrated in trying to communicate with humans. There are many barriers on our part, such as lack of "hearing," disbelief, physical-plane preoccupations, and incompatabilities in vibration levels. The newly deceased are often shouting at their earthly loved ones and companions that they're fine now and not to grieve. They also try to convey urgent advices (like love one another) but often humans don't hear. (Many spiritual traditions note that small children can often more easily receive such messages.)

There is a curious thing with many tantalizing implications. Humans can help disembodied spirits, too. We can help free low-level and earthbound spirits by communicating with them with kindness and understanding. We can let go of the ones we're still emotionally tied to so that they can more freely proceed on their own way. But aside from these things, it seems that our growth in awareness "leaks" to spirits we are connected with, and they share in our expansion. We are also data and experience gatherers for them. So our relationships with the discarnate are two-way and mutually beneficial.

Awe of disembodied spirits is fading in our time. More and more people are getting into conscious communication with them and drawing on them for assistance and guidance and even simple companionship. So discarnate spirits are playing an important, reciprocal part in the worldwide awakening movement.

Someone recently asked me what the best single word to describe spirit was. I knew immediately that no one word would really do. But, for what it's worth, the word that leaped into my mind to catch the essence of spirits at all levels of evolvement was *playful*.

6

The Beyond

Our familiar physical plane is only a very thin slice, a tiny portion of All That Is. This fact raises immediate curiosity about all the other planes, places, and dimensions. What are they like? What's going on there?

In the last two decades we've learned more than we ever knew before, about many things. This includes the Beyond. But when we try to understand the Beyond we run into a basic, unresolvable problem. The problem is this, and there's no way around it: The Beyond is *not describable* in rational, left-brain human terms. All those reporting direct experiences with the Beyond begin by emphatically stating that it is verbally indescribable. They use analogies and metaphors ("It's like . . . ") to try to convey what they have experienced. But, they hasten to add that these descriptions are entirely inadequate ("You would just have to have been there . . . "). The realities of "the other side" are evidently far beyond what's described in our wildest science fiction and fantasy novels, although these are sometimes based on glimpses of them. So everything we say about these other planes can only be suggestive hints.

If here is here and the Beyond is beyond, where does our data come from? Actually, there are many sources when one begins to look. We now have the detailed accounts of many hundreds of NDEs, gathered by Moody, Ring, Kubler-Ross, Flynn, and many others. From Wambach and Whitton, among others, we have the case histories of hundreds of subjects who were regressed to the between-lives period (following past deaths and prior to further births). There also are many reports from psychic adepts who have travelled these realms in out-of-body experiences. There are mystic tracts such as the *Tibetan Book of the Dead* (remarkably paralleling contemporary reports) and the Kabbalah. More recently, there are Robert Monroe's *Far Journeys*, and descriptions from a growing number of channeled disembodied spirits, notably Seth, Michael, Orin, and Enid. So we do have something to go on.

Our available descriptions of the Beyond vary to some extent and are not altogether consistent. There are two good reasons for these variations. First, there is the individual's own belief system, which greatly colors the reporting person's translation and interpretation of the raw experience. A devout Christian, a Buddhist, a science fiction fan, and a lover of fairy tales would each translate a raw Beyond experience somewhat differently and draw different meanings from it. The traveller's tale, when brought back, always reflects the mindset of the traveller, to some degree.

The second source of variation in reports arises from the vast and variegated nature of the Beyond itself. To be accurate, we probably should be using the plural—the Beyonds. To begin with, there are many levels in the spiritual realms, in increasing refinement of what we might crudely call vibration level or wavelength. Much like the variations in a color spectrum, these represent degrees of refinement of spirit. The lower ones are the coarsest and most similar to those of our physical plane. The higher levels evidently become increasingly "heavenly," in every sense of the word. There are also different "locales" with their own distinctive, unearthly features in the astral planes. There are meadows, lakes, forests, glittering cities, crystal spires, and other types of imaginable landscape, as well as some unimaginable ones. Movement from one area to another is by will or intention, although one must be able to manifest the matching wavelengths to move "vertically" up or down the levels. Many of the mythical places in our literature draw their inspiration from actual realities on the astral levels. And all this is only one system among many many different systems, dimensions, and other physical and nonphysical realities. You may yet have a chance to visit your favorite fairyland or mythic place.

There is a great deal of luminescence on most levels of the spiritual realms, but this is not ordinary light. It seems to have almost a living quality, inherently containing such properties as warmth and understanding and love. Indeed, knowledge and wisdom on these levels seem to be "in the air" and open to everyone. No one is disqualified from being anywhere, except temporarily, by reason of their own considerations. In other words, there are no doctrinaire judgments about who is or is not okay. Our human sectarianism is not evident. Herald Sherman, the pioneer psychic researcher, recounts one newly deceased spirit telling a relative, "It's not like the preachers say it is."

The lowest astral realms are reported to be dim and dismal. Their greyness and squalor is created by the beliefs and images of the inhabitants. Here abide spirits still very much tied to addictions of the earthly plane and those yet manifesting a coarser, denser vibration level. They are in every sense more distant from the Light. The experience of these lower realms is like that of going into a sleazy bar after being on a beautiful beach all day. But these levels are not the hells of human conception, nor is anyone condemned to stay there forever. Beings can and do leave when they are ready, through personal growth, for the higher realms. Also they are frequently rescued by higher level beings.

Communication among inhabitants of the Beyonds is direct, and nonverbal, and therefore free from verbal misunderstandings and deceptions. This direct transference is not only of thoughts; it is also the sharing of feelings, emotions, attitudes, and experiences. The sharing is voluntary, as is almost everything else. Evidently, discarnate beings also use these abilities to read the inner thoughts, feelings, and past histories of incarnate humans.

Although newly arrived and mid-level beings may manifest themselves in male and female forms, all reports agree that there is no gender among spirits. More highly evolved spirits have succeeded in integrating both male and female attributes and energies (yin and yang) as part of their transcendental development. Astral beings can, however, manifest gender or some other characteristic if they so wish.

For example, they will sometimes appear to humans in male or female form.

There is no physical sex in the Beyond, but there is spiritual togetherness and vibrational sensualities that are, reputedly, "the real thing". These sensualities encompass a far wider range of energy interchanges and sensations than physical love-making. So any ideas that the spiritual realms are drab, thin, or prim is simply not true, according to the reports. These realms are rich in experiences, emotions, sensations, wonders, adventures, and beauties.

The substance making up the astral realms is of a far finer essence than physical-plane matter, so one's thoughts and intentions can more directly and swiftly shape it. In other words, Creative Visualization works swiftly and powerfully to produce the forms of a spirit's imagination, without the toils and tools usually needed for physical-plane productions. Among the newly deceased, this results in the temporary persistence of ethereal versions of earthly forms. These include bodies, familiar settings, even food and drink, manifested by astral matter responding directly to wishes and will. Such forms often also include self-fulfilling creations reflecting the being's previous beliefs about the afterlife. So there are temporary manifestations of Valhalla, Paradise, Heaven, and the Happy Hunting Grounds. These fade out or are transmuted as the being begins to understand the realities underlying the spiritual (and all other) realms. As this occurs, ties to the physical plane also fade.

This might all sound rather far-fetched. But these unearthly sketches come from hard-bitten construction workers, self-indulgent wastrels, prim schoolteachers, children, and Yuppies, who had never heard of Tibetan mysticism, but who transformed their lives after a spiritual awakening. And they come, also, from spiritual seekers of the highest order, admired by millions. So these accounts are worth pondering.

A virtually unanimous theme in the accounts is that the Beyond is *friendly*. In near-death and out-of-body experiences, some people report temporary disorientation and upset. But this is soon after washed away by the ambience of the Other Side and by the loving greetings from other beings. Despairing communications from some discarnate spirits have been reported, but their content and other evidence suggest that these emanated from earthbound spirits who had not yet kicked free from their physical-plane preoccupations and obsessions. The simple but profound truth seems to be that All That Is is ultimately a vast cooperative endeavor on the part of all consciousnesses.

A good many religions and cults claim to be the exclusive travel agents and gatekeepers for the Afterlife. However, all our sources agree that this is not the case. Anybody can go there and everybody does.

When a spirit separates from the body at the time of physical death, it usually finds itself drawn into the Beyond. The radical shift in perspective resulting from the disembodied state, plus the astral peace and warmth and the greetings from other spirits, usually provide enough impetus to separate from the physical plane with its worries, pains, and attachments. There also seems to be a rapid shift to a cosmic viewpoint about mundane things, which further helps to lift the being above the concerns and denser vibration levels of the physical life just departed from. This all has something of the nature of a joyous homecoming.

Some beings linger "near" the earthly plane for a cosmic moment or two, appearing to loved ones to reassure them, or even attending their own funerals. This "near" level interpenetrates with the physical plane so the discarnate can clearly perceive what's going on here, but is usually not consciously sensed by humans. Such a being already possesses some of the inherent spirit abilities to move at will and to psychically impinge on humans, perhaps in dreams.

Not all beings go through this earthly tidying up period, and for most of those who do, it is usually short. A compulsive attachment to some person, place, or thing can, however, prolong the transition period. A dying mother, for example, might not let go of a child she is obsessively attached to (and herself dependent upon). But the pull "upward" into the luminous astral realms is somewhat irresistible, so that these kinds of clinging fixations are eventually transcended. Since the spirit realms are timeless, at least in our ordinary wristwatch understanding of time, such transitional lingerings are really only a blink in the cosmic scheme of things.

Physical death is usually experienced as a release and a relief, something like taking off a shoe that's too tight at the end of the day. This may be mixed with a lingering sadness over leaving loved ones behind and a compassionate sensing of their grief. If the life was uncommonly drab, harsh, or boring, the being is especially pleased that it is now over. The being is up and away, both locationally and psychologically. All of the conditions of the Beyond seem to combine to create states which have been variously named superconsciousness, meta-consciousness, and cosmic consciousness. Whatever these states are, they obviously encompass a profound spiritual awakening.

The new astral arrival may initially be overcome with surprise and confusion at its "new" surroundings, but other beings appear to lead and reassure the spirit and help it get oriented. Greetings from old companions are warm and loving. Aside from beings of light, the welcomers include friends, relatives, lovers, and members of one's spiritual "family," all familiar from the just-ended or previous lifetimes. It seems that beings sometimes wait around for each other after discorporating. The discorporate who have gone before often act as guides and guardians for the people still incarnate until they "pass on." These are probably a main source of the guardian angel stories, and the intuitions and precognitions that often accompany them. In many cases, they also may be the imaginary playmates that some children claim to have.

What do beings *do* in the Beyond? The new arrival has become a bit acclimated and has recaptured some of its inherent spiritual abilities—what next? For those recently deceased, but who are still involved in successive reincarnations, there is first a time of R and R, of rest and revitalization. It is often a period of recuperation from the life just ended, a sort of rotation from the combat zone. The interactions with the beings one has known before are exceptionally pleasurable, because the human barriers are absent. There is often a sort of vacation touring of various astral locales, an enjoyment of the beauties and adventures to be found. Also there are the enlightenments gained from a panoramic review of past lives, in which one can see and learn from the karmic consequences on oneself and others of one's in-human actions and inactions. There are chances for consultation with wiser spirits and a very extensive educational curriculum. Also, one can pursue any of the creative arts or crafts.

Seemingly, there is no lack of wondrous things to do. Beings who have transcended physical-plane reincarnations are busy pursuing their further spiritual development and helping less evolved beings. Evidently these tasks are joyous and provide more than enough challenges and pleasures.

There are realms above realms on the spiritual plane. The higher they are, the more incomprehensible to mortals they would seem to be, these high realms that are beyond the Beyond. But lest we feel cowed and dwarfed before such a cosmic view of things, it is well to remember that virtually all spiritual traditions assert that each of us carries within ourselves a living essence that is intimately connected with All That Is, and so we are never lost.

For those souls still going through a reincarnational phase of development, the stay in the Beyond is a temporary between-lives sojourn. How long between incarnations? Helen Wambach, the eminent past-lives therapist, did a statistical analysis of over eleven hundred past-life regressions cases in which the reported period ranged from four months to more than two hundred years. The average (mean) was fifty-two years. Michael says that younger souls (in terms of evolvement) tend to rush back into physical life. Young soldiers killed in battle also usually return quickly. Older souls linger longer on the astral levels to do business before returning.

It seems that the decision to be reborn is self-determined by each being in consultation with familiar spirits and, often, a small group of more knowledgeable counsellors. The rebirth is planned, except for those spirits who just rush back on the basis of physical-plane addictions. Such plans include the circumstances of birth and a blueprint outline of the life to follow, so that certain experiences might provide the opportunity to learn certain lessons. The plans include, for example, some details about geographical region, gender, family to be born into, and the life companions one is likely to have. The plannings also set up possible opportunities to "work things out" with certain other beings with whom one has karmic connections and indebtednesses.

These between-lives plans for the upcoming physical life have a Grand Design flavor. They are more far-seeing than earthly planning usually is, and are made from a more transcendental viewpoint. However, they are not infallible. For one thing, discarnate beings tend to forget the raw, dense-wavelength intensity of physical-plane life. So in their agendas they will sometimes bite off more than they later wish to chew. Also, the vaulting distance from the current details of physical-plane realities seems to produce miscalculations. For example, economic conditions may be changing in some chosen geographic area. Or one of the intended major life companions may be about to suffer a setback that will introduce unforeseen changes. Or a chosen city may have gone through unrecognized changes, such as a massive flight to the suburbs or shifts in ethnic makeup. In all incarnating journeys there seems to be an inevitable difference between planning for the trip and actually taking the trip. This, again, points up the important fact that disembodied beings do not know everything and are themselves still evolving.

If life plans go astray during the actual incarnation, there are always things the being can do to gain experience and wisdom. That is, the being can and does improvise with whatever materials and circumstances are at hand. After all, *every consciousness is ultimately a creative artist*. However, the failing of the original plans often leaves the person with vague, persistent feelings of being off the track, alienated from the circumstances encountered. During that lifetime, the in-human may feel like a stranger in a strange land, never quite at home.

According to Wambach's extensive data, the attitudes of those in the between-lives state, prior to being born, varied from eagerness to ambivalence to reluctance. But among them all there was a common "here we go again" feeling, a bit like standing in line waiting to go on a roller coaster ride. A sense of a major purpose for the coming life was almost universal among her regressed subjects, although some weren't at that time clear on exactly what it was. The recalled purposes were quite varied: to master some ability, overcome some personal flaw, fill in certain experiences, help specific other persons, gain some physical knowledge, work through a fear of loving and giving, better some world situation, be in on the women's movement, and so on.

During the pregnancy the spirit hovers around the fetus and the mother, and settles into the new body around the time of birth. Soon after birth, however, the meta-consciousness of most begins to fade and a clear spiritual awareness starts to get buried beneath the necessity to focus on the demands of the new life situations. Considering where they have just come from, it is true in a sense that a child can be "heaven sent," as expressed in so many popular songs. Also one of the reasons children are usually so bushy-tailed may be that they've just had a good rest. It may also be no accident that children are particularly entranced with fairy tales and other stories of magical realms. They may dimly recall being there.

Those still involved in successive incarnations seem to occupy a middle ground, with those "below" not yet up to rebirth and those "above" having graduated into higher spirals of evolvement. However, beings at all stages share the ultimate universal brotherhood of spirits.

Inhabitants of the Beyond are able from their vantage point to perceive what is going on with physical-plane conditions and persons. This seems to be something of a one-way mirror situation; they can see us, but we can hardly perceive them, if at all, although we may subliminally sense them. We've seen that all paranormal phenomena are spiritually based. The corollary of this is that discarnate spirits all possess ESP in their sensings of any environment. From the available reports, such perceptions are not complete nor always accurate, but they are impressive.

Not surprisingly, the evolvement level of the being is the main factor in determining the depth and scope of such perceptions, but all discarnates have some of these abilities. The lowest astral levels resemble more a spiritual skid row than they do the hell of traditional religions. The inhabitants have a correspondingly low consciousness level and perceive the earth plane poorly, although they may claim high psychic abilities and magical powers. According to Roman and Packer, the Frosts, Bethayes, and other veteran psychic researchers, the ordinary incarnate human is usually more conscious and perceptive than they are. Mid-level beings are impressive but limited in their perceptions of our plane. Their powers of perception might be roughly equivalent to those of in-human mystics and spiritual adepts.

High level beings can only be described as awesome in the vast scope and detail of their perceptions of the earth plane. The knowledge manifested about particular individuals or particular world events by Seth, or Michael, or Orin is simply uncanny and has been verified again and again. They can also tell you more than you may want to know about esoteric subjects like fourteenth-century Cambodian art, or obscure historical events such as the migrations of the Parthians.

In-humans also have their perceptions of the spiritual realms. These are often experienced in deep sleep states, although they are seldom recognized. Astral travel has also been a common underground tradition in both East and West, and techniques for doing this are now being widely disseminated as part of the New Age awakening.

Spiritually evolved people throughout history have not been afraid of death because they recalled or directly experienced something of the astral planes. Such knowledge, even if slight, can cause a dramatic shift in perspectives on dying.

From the foregoing, it would seem a mistake to think of the physical and spiritual realms as being mutually opposing, or to reject one in favor of the other. Both play their parts in the spiritual evolutionary scheme. To deny the physical realm is to turn one's back on the experiences we are here to learn, and to guarantee that we will continue to return until we "do the course" and graduate. To deny the spiritual realms is to deny *our own essential natures* and to miss the fact that only spirits can transform the mundane and touch it with some magic.

As indescribable as the Beyond may be, there is one comforting thought about it: We'll all get to discover it for ourselves.

7

Messages From Beyond

Well, if there's all this interchange between disembodied spirits and humans, what do the spirits have to say? If you could ask any question of a wise discarnate spirit, what would you ask? It seems that virtually every kind of question has been asked at one time or another, from what kind of car to buy, and whether one's spouse is being unfaithful, to the meaning of life. And the spirits have responded —sometimes saying more than the person bargained for, and sometimes with refusals to answer on the grounds that the inquirers needed to learn for themselves.

There are now tens of thousands of reports of communications and advices from discarnates. Sorting through a large sample of such cases, you find quite a variation in both content and level. However, there are some remarkable similarities among the messages, regardless of time, place, and circumstance.

The overwhelming majority of all the reported messages are positive, helpful, and uplifting. The small fraction of upsetting, negative, and dire communications emanate from low astral and earthbound beings who are themselves troubled. For example, a deceased former tenant angrily communicated, "Get out of my house," to the new owners, until her problem was resolved. A low-level astral being hung around a sleazy motel, encouraging the overnight guests to "go wild." Once, on a mountain lookout spot in northern California, the spirit of an Indian, still enraged at the "white eyes" who caused his death and the destruction of his family, kept telling me to "jump."

These and similar messages are not compelling. In fact, they only have the power you grant them because of some resonance they may currently have with you. If a human acquaintance told you to jump off a building, you certainly wouldn't. Such negative impingements can be easily handled by mentally brushing them aside, or by telling the spirit to go away, or by calling upon higher level beings for help. One can also communicate with and help lower level spirits through their travails. Often they only want to tell their story and be understood and accepted. They are then able to move along on their own path of development. In any case they are only a small part of the paranormal story, which has been far too overblown in popular novels and movies. As the world famous psychic, Edgar Cayce, pointed out, they are learning and evolving just like you and me. Your greatest defense against such negative thoughtforms is your own healthy mind and body—and expanded consciousness.

Low-level discarnates will sometimes attempt to instill fright into humans. They might broadcast images of a red-eyed monster waiting to get you in the basement, or fears that some enterprise is going to be a disaster. In the middle of the night such a spirit came toward me manifesting as a werewolf, complete with dripping teeth and claws. I went over to him, gave him a hug, and asked him to scratch my itching back with his claws. He chittered in amazement and melted away. Incidentally, for some reason, the use of a small nightlight will forestall most such nightime visitations. Children, being more wide open psychically, are more prone to such impingements. So if a child (or grownup) is afraid of the dark, just give him or her a little light.

Setting these low-level impingements aside, the largest number of spirit messages are specific personal greetings, advice, and admonitions from friends and loved ones who have "passed on." Although these are usually very meaningful to the recipients, they often seem trivial to those of us who are not involved. "Remember to clean the gutters before the spring rains come." "Don't get involved in that business deal with Bill; he's untrustworthy." "Don't worry, George will make you a good husband." "Stop fretting about me; I don't have any more pain and it's beautiful here. I love you and I'll see you before too long now." Such messages are often touching, even poignant, but not all that remarkable except for their *sources*. The venerable psychic investigator Harold Sherman's books are filled with documentations of such communications, many of which contain details only the deceased would know. According to Andrew Greeley's ongoing, Chicago-based, National Opinion Research Center survey, a large percent of widows and widowers reported such communications from their deceased spouses although they didn't tell their doctors. And Elizabeth Kubler-Ross found that dying children with one foot already in the spiritual realms often take up the task of comforting and reassuring their distressed families.

These kinds of messages often provide solace and reassurance and continuing support for humans in need, and the evidence for their validity is now massive. To dismiss them as wish-fulfilling fantasies is neither scientific nor humane.

Higher Level Guides

In recent years, most attention has been given to the outpouring of messages from higher level guides and channeled spirits. There is now a very extensive literature published by the in-human partners of these discarnates. And for every channelled spirit whose messages reach print or public notice, there are many more who are unreported. For example, there are channels in the Philippine jungles and the mountains of Peru and in small midwestern towns that you'll probably never hear about. The spirit messages don't always agree about specific issues, such as suicide, but such disagreements seem to reflect either the evolvement level of the spirit or the possible biases of the recipients as they translate the images received into human terms. In spite of these variations, however, a remarkable degree of agreement is manifested.

The common messages from more evolved spirits present a paradox. They usually are simple to state but difficult to grasp, because they seem so above and beyond our daily physical-plane experiences and entrancements. For example, try practicing unconditional love for a day, or embracing the idea that your beliefs create the realities you experience! Also they sometimes seem to be a one-hundred-eighty-degree turnaround from our mainstream cultural beliefs and prevailing religious dogmas. For example, their messages often tell us that the courses of our current lives are partly an unfolding of plans we made in concert with others before our births. The first time we encounter notions like this, through books or in a group workshop, we might feel they are too bizarre and too cute. But in time they can grow on us. Also, feelings that they are goodie-two-shoes may reflect, in fact, the depths of our own current negative programming and coarse vibration level manifestation.

Some of the common themes expressed in these transcendent communications are included in the list of basic premises at the end of Chapter One. But there are more.

Here is a composite sketch of "the real story" according to these beings. The cosmos—All That Is—is composed of an unthinkable number of different dimensions and different realities, all cooperatively created by Consciousness. Consciousness is continuously evolving everywhere. Realities differ endlessly and inconceivably, but each is a valid illusion. Earth School is one of many realities set up for accelerated learning, experience, and growth.

All consciousness is simultaneously independent and individual, but also inherently interconnected; each consciousness being a part of All That Is and All That Is being the collective expression of all consciousness.

From our spiritual underpinnings, through the creative manifestation of our beliefs and intentions, we create the realities we experience. Collectively we co-author Earth realities. Different ethnic groups literally create and inhabit different worlds within the larger planetary sphere. We are all performers in the melodramas we have co-created and staged.

Individual consciousness has free choice. It *must* have free choice in order to evolve and for All That Is to work. In the universal scheme of things, each individual consciousness is considered far more precious and of far more worth than we usually grant to ourselves or others. *All* life is sacred. However, the "worship" of more evolved spirits by less evolved ones is a perverse form of self-denial. Thankfulness, on the other hand, is a warm, positive vibration of appreciation, and an affirmation of our interconnections that creates more inter-spirit warmth.

Quality of life is much more important than mere survival. A being will decide to terminate its incarnation in a particular physical life form when the quality of life is no longer suitable for its purposes. According to this viewpoint, beings always decide when to terminate life cycles. No exceptions.

More evolved consciousnesses watch over and assist the less evolved in a caring nurturance. This is not intervention, which would limit free choice, but the providing of enriched opportunities which a less evolved being can utilize or not as it chooses. This assistance is not a matter of duty, but of enjoyment. (Remember the enjoyment of helping someone with no strings attached?). It is also an outlet for creative expression and an avenue for further experience for the more highly evolved. So everybody wins.

In the multidimensional scheme of things, every individual consciousness has the chance to experience just about anything and everything it desires and needs for its growth. So if you want to be a successful entrepreneur for a lifetime, or a wanton, or the guardian of a forest, or a spaceship captain, or a sensitive psychic, you will have chances to do so. So have heart. And you also can arrange to enjoy a restful vacation from it all.

All of this might sound quite un-American and un-Christian at first blush. But I like to think of it as meta-American and meta-Christian. This too, of course, is a matter of free choice.

Messages About Our Personal Needs

What about our personal *human* situations and turmoils and

problems? Channeled advice is often specific to the person asking and their particular circumstances, but even here the generic lofty viewpoint manifests itself. The beings usually won't supply pat directives; that is, they won't just tell you what to do. They are more like a good math teacher who will help you with the problems but not take the exams for you. The help is only help because individual consciousnesses *must* learn for themselves so that they may evolve.

A main theme of their messages is that our civilization and the individuals within it have become grossly out of balance and that, to live better, these balances should be restored. It is strongly suggested that we restore intuition as a guide in living, not to banish logic but to integrate it with intuitions which are rooted in our spiritual connections. This means looking inward, as well as (not instead of) looking outward. They tell us that we could live more happily if we listened to the heart as well as the head.

We are enjoined to be our own gurus. We are anyway, so we might as well be conscious and accepting of the fact. This involves a nourishing and celebration of Selfhood with a continuing growth of independence and self-determinism. There's no paradox in the fact that this goes along with a growth in awareness of and connectedness with all other consciousnesses.

Such notions, increasingly, are transforming millions of lives.

MESSAGES ABOUT LOVE

Love is said to be the strongest force, the strongest vibration, in all the cosmos, but this idea is not an easy one for incarnate humans to fully grasp. Love supposedly has more "flavors" and manifestations than all of the other emotions combined.

The highest level of love, for self and others and all things, is superior in its power to fear or negativity. It transcends exchange considerations or "keeping score." This love must be distinguished from the physical attractions and lusts usually expressed in popular songs, novels, and movies, although such attractions can transmute into a higher love. It is neither dominating nor submissive; it embodies neither claims nor jealousies; it is itself and unconditional. The most familiar physical-plane example that sometimes approaches this is the unconditional love of some parents for their children, whatever they become and however they turn out. In a milder form, most of us have had the experience of simply liking some people no matter what they do. It seems that part of everyone's spiritual evolvement is sooner or later to learn to consistently manifest this level of love and compassion.

The evidence from thousands of reports of near-death experiences suggests that discarnate beings who are helpers practice what they preach. Those who have returned say that they were greeted by Beings of Light who enveloped them in luminous waves of non-judgmental love and understanding. They further report that the experiencing of this love transcended any sensual experiences of their physical lives. Consequently, many of them were not entirely happy about returning to the earth plane.

This vaulting conception of unconditional love seems the hardest message to understand, let alone to live by. Yet it is the most universal communication of all from Beyond. In following the path to such exalted love, we are told, the heart is wiser than the mind.

There are other common themes of advice, although these are seldom in the form of "shoulds." There are no "right" or "wrong" choices from a cosmic viewpoint, but there are *better* choices. There is the common suggestion that it is rewarding to seek spiritual *and* mundane knowledge, wisdom, and growth. It is not recommended that we withdraw from the world, except in special circumstances and temporarily, because we are here to gather the lessons of the physical plane. There is little or no suggestion that we give up our enjoyment of material things, but there is a strong common theme about not being obsessed with the material to the neglect of things spiritual. "Open our spiritual eyes."

Each of us has his or her own path which will be unique in some respects. At any given time we must choose the sources of knowledge and experience that seem intuitively right, moving on to other books, disciplines, and scenarios when the time comes. Wisdom is where we find it, and our soul remembers what we've learned and goes on from there.

We are encouraged to serve and care for one another. But it is *not* good work to foist care upon someone who does not want it at the time, or to try to force people to convert to our way "for their own good." These are two hard lessons to learn and live by, because most of us tend to be zealots about our own points of view.

Serving should not be dutiful or demanding either for giver or receiver, otherwise there are too many strings involved. Nor does serving need to be grand or grandiose. It can be as simple as being cheerful toward one another. More broadly, it involves seeking Win-Win scenerios in which our profit is not someone else's loss. Extreme selfishness produces its own backlash. Advisory spirits point out that saying this isn't moralizing; it reflects one of the "natural laws" of how energy interchanges between beings work.

Caring for others (in both senses of the word) has nothing to do with propitiation or self-sacrifice either. Such emotions often reflect deep-seated feelings of low self-worth. If we first learn to care for ourselves, everyone benefits. The fact is, everyone has incalculable worth.

When we sense our interconnectedness with all the other beings and things in the cosmos, we operate quite differently than when we perceived ourselves as separate and socially distant from them. The "battle of the sexes," race relations, and international negotiations all take on a different flavor and have different outcomes. It is interesting that the planetary ecologists and environmentalists have, from different lines of reasoning, come up with similar conclusions. We all share the biosphere together and share one another's breaths and flower scents and exhaust fumes.

Messages About Creating Our Realities

I did an informal content analysis of about 150 reported direct messages of personal advice from high-level discarnates and found that one factor stood out, expressed in many different ways. *We create the realities we experience, consciously or unknowingly*. The universe ultimately gives us what we ask for. This holds for all dimensions and all levels of the cosmos. Since we construct our own lives, it is false and misleading to blame others for what we are experiencing. We are not pawns in some cosmic saga, but active producers, directors, and co-authors. The buck stops with us. And change is in our own hands. We all engage continually in positive or negative Creative Visualization (imaging) that is utterly successful.

This is not just a matter of our outward actions and the environment's responses. Our internal beliefs and thought-forms become manifested as the world we inhabit and experience. As Orin/Sanaya Roman says, if you change your mind you change your future.

One crucial aspect of this process is the devastating effect of negative thought forms and negative vibration wavelengths. Leading-edge research now suggests that there is a negative self-programming component to every illness (dis-ease) and accident. *Vibrational Medicine*, by Richard Gerber, M.D. and *Love, Medicine, and Miracles*, by Bernie Siegel, M.D. are filled with illustrations of this point. Listen to someone's conversation for a few minutes and you are likely to hear a whole stream of negative, critical, ominous, pessimistic, and self-deprecating statements. Listen to your own stream of thoughts for a minute and you may hear similar things.

At the interpersonal level, negative comments and vibrations are like stray bullets ricocheting through the social environment. They also can be looked at as a psychic plague sweeping over the planet. This is a painful and unnecessary way to learn the lessons of the physical plane. The idea that suffering is somehow ennobling is itself a perverse negative belief. Plants and people do best in a rich, luxuriant environment.

High-level spirits invite us to become full masters of ourselves; to be ever more conscious and self-determined in following our own path and calling our own shots. Be inner-directed. Learn to hear and trust your own heart, your own inner guidance. For starters, these spirits don't want you to be dependent on *them*, because this would impede rather than encourage spiritual growth. They promote understanding without condemning anyone, including those who refuse the understanding at this time. Their acceptance of everyone, wherever they are currently at, does, in fact, seem supernatural.

A final frequent message is that real happiness on the physical plane happens only at the higher vibration levels, those which are positive and which encompass some degree of spiritual contact and awareness. Without these qualities there is no magic, and incarnate life is almost inevitably somewhat drab, grey, and painful, with a few occasional pleasurable sensations thrown in. The difference between trauma and adventure is largely a matter of the consciousness level of the experiencer.

THE CHANNELING OF MESSAGES

These messages of advice weave together into a coherent pattern that forms part of the manifesto of the spiritual awakening movement. They are not altogether easy to follow. They may even seem glib — at least until we try to apply them in daily living. We may then quickly discover how far above current human doings they really are.

In recent years there has been a tremendous increase in the channeling of spirit messages. There are now courses and books on how to become a channel, such as Roman and Packard's *Opening to Channel*. Supposedly, as the amount of channeling increases it becomes easier for even more channeling to occur, in a snowballing effect. Some folks have predicted that spirit channeling will become a normal everyday practice within a few generations. Well, the future has *always* been a surprise.

However, it can be risky business for people who are not very spiritually evolved to seek to become channels. Someone who chronically manifests only coarse, low-level wavelengths is likely to connect only with lesser-evolved spirits because of the Like Attracts Like law. So while we are emotionally and spiritually unstable, it is better to first work on our own balancing and spiritual development.

There obviously are some communication problems between humans and disembodied spirits; otherwise there would be far more conscious communication, although there is much more than we once thought. In the first place, the more highly evolved spirit must step down its vibrational wavelength, while humans must step theirs up. Also, it seems that the vibrational qualities must be somewhat resonant or harmonious for decent transmission to occur. Evidently, like attracts like in the realm of spirit connections and messages, too.

If the human is not open to such communications, the messages will be ignored or blocked, often through disbelief or fear. Disbelief stems from the fantastic nature of the connection. The fear may be of the unknown, of being taken over, of being naked before another being. A gentle, negotiated buildup of trust and camaraderie must be worked up for these to be overcome. The results can be indescribably rewarding.

Even among the most willing recipients, there is the transmission limitation of the human's mental language and concept structure. Just as we might have trouble communicating the principles of aerodynamics to an island native who lacks a scientific conceptual framework, so a high-level spirit can only communicate the concepts and ideas which the individuals are equipped by their knowledge and belief systems to receive. This is probably why spirits so often communicate by means of analogies, symbols, and images. Some high-level notions simply cannot be translated into human terms.

High-level beings employ a wide variety of means to communicate with incarnate humans. They often come to us in dreams, although all dreams are certainly not such messages. They also make subtle subliminal suggestions, or subtly reinforce certain of our own thoughts and feelings. They inseminate intuitions and inspirations. They can make some adjustments in the energy fields in and around our bodies. They can lead others to influence us. To some degree they can evidently manipulate events, leading us to find a certain book or to meet a certain person. But the individual remains free to override or refuse these influences. (Low-level humans and those trapped in addictions, however, may lack the free will to resist such impingements.) Also, their influencing actions are limited by their own "code" of providing opportunities but not compelling. It seems to be one of their guiding principles that free choice remains in our hands.

Just because a message comes from a disembodied spirit is no guarantee that it is wise or even correct advice for all humans. Since spirits vary even more than humans in their degree of experience and evolvement, their messages also vary in these same qualities. Spirits have their own "trips" to push, that reflect their own background and stage of development. Mid-level spirits sometimes moralize and sermonize, echoing their earthly beliefs and ethnic backgrounds in some cases. In the case of higher level guides, this lessens and fades. For example, lower level spirits say suicide is a sin, while higher level ones say the spirit *always* chooses when it leaves the body. Dire, threatening, or dreadful messages are always either from less evolved beings or they are one's own projections.

PREDICTING THE FUTURE

What about the future? Will the spirits predict for us? No, not really.

One of the most common requests from humans is for the spirits to tell them their future. Occasional predictions are made, but the requests are essentially refused for two reasons. First, predictions rob people of choices and make them dependent, which violates the reasons for being here. But there is a second, deeper reason. There is no predestination, no immutable future to predict. Particular lines of action lead to certain probable futures which can evidently be easily seen from an astral perspective. But there are no sure bets. As people change their thoughts and actions, the future shifts. We (and they) are free from the tyranny of any Fate. Our life is in our own hands.

High-level spirits seem keenly interested in assisting the spiritual awakening movement. Will they help lead us into a gentler, sweeter age? We'll see.

8

Spirit & Circumstance

As you look around the world you might conclude that most people are not manifesting much spirituality in their lives. Or if they are, it is mostly in a devious and obscure manner, hidden even from themselves. Why doesn't the light of their deathless spiritual essence come shining through for all to see? What's going on here?

On the earthly plane, there is a fact that cannot be avoided and that has enormous implications for every being residing here. Social scientists have well documented how every human being is deeply trained in the ways and beliefs of his or her family, community, and society. The layer upon layer extensiveness, intensity, and depth of this social programming are hard for us to really grasp, because we are immersed in it, like a fish is always immersed in water. We can easily see the stamp of this deep socialization on every member of a group. For instance, even the criminals, the mentally disturbed, and fringe group members raised in this country are recognizably late-twentieth-century Americans, who never would be mistaken for someone raised in Mongolia or Burma. Hundreds of studies have shown that people tend to have political, religious, social, and economic beliefs and practices remarkably similar to those of their parents. This is partly how it comes about that each family, each community, each region, and each country has its own distinctive collective aura or psychic vibration pattern. (There is also the Like Attracts Like rule operating in this similarity, as we've seen.) *To be accepted as a full member in a society, an individual must learn and manifest the collective wisdom, values, attitudes, distortions, and negativities of the group.*

As beings hunker down into the physical plane, and their

panoramic metaconsciousness fades, they are usually disoriented and confused, at least to the extent of wondering, "Where am I?" In such a state, a being is literally impressionable to the deliberate and incidental programming every group puts new members through. Through this heavy orientation process, the being learns about the circumstances surrounding it—but it may also learn to be submissive, to be afraid of ghosts, or to believe that things are more real than thoughts. Because individuals then act out this programming, it becomes somewhat self-fulfilling and "true" in their lives. Those who have been more or less successfully programmed then work to similarly program the rest of the population, in their roles as parents, teachers, and companions. And after a while, the mask becomes the face.

One might say the person is under a spell, en-tranced. Circumstances tend to deeply introvert the incarnated spirit into whatever local games are going on. This can tie up most of the person's attention and energy to the point that the person may feel this is all there is, like a plowman who never looks up to see the horizon. Individuals can get almost entirely immersed in a physical-plane *identity*, just like a child becoming totally lost in a card game. This is perhaps the ultimate in tunnel vision. The person's perspectives may dwindle to the point where he or she goes through a round of ritualized, treadmill activities: going to work, making some money, buying some food, and resting; going to work, making some money, and so on. Even a person's contemplations, daydreams, and fantasies may be mostly locked up in current circumstantial games and personalities.

There is, of course, a very positive and necessary side to a being's circumstances. They provide the scenery and props and other players for the games the person is wittingly or unwittingly playing. Through circumstance one has roads and buildings and food and local culture; through circumstance (but not coincidence) one meets a friend, a collaborator on some task, a lover, an antagonist one can hassle with. Circumstances also provide movie theatres, ice cream, a peaceful lake, an exciting bar, and a level of maintenance, high or low, for the organin which the being is biologically based. Circumstances provide the skeletal blueprints and the raw materials for the games that result in learning experiences. And circumstances always provide the potential triggers for spiritual awakening.

This is Earth School.

The Entrancement of the Physical Plane

If it was actually true that a human being is no more than a biological machine, then the programming from our social surroundings would be completely effective and we would be no more than passive, dutiful cogs in a mechanical universe. But this is never the case! Socialization, no matter how rigidly or forcefully it is carried out, is never infallible and never entirely successful, as any despairing parent or dictator can tell you. Because there is a spirit energizing the body, the person, the "I", always remains to some degree an active agent. One of the most frustrating but exciting things about human beings is that you can never be utterly certain about what they will think or do. People can be assigned roles and taught the expectations that go along with them, but the person will always do some active shaping and improvising in their actual performances. Within the range of available circumstances, individuals will do some of their own choosing about who to admire and who to ignore. And they will make some of their own deals on the basis of their own inner calculations of costs and rewards.

Influence there certainly is, but it flows in both directions. Local circumstances and programming color the being's experiences on the physical plane, but at the same time the being is actively helping to shape and color these same physical plane surroundings. There is also the fact that the being actively chooses his or her circumstances, either consciously or obsessively.

All of this is "good" from the viewpoint that we are here to fully experience the physical plane and to learn and evolve through these experiences. New Age writers mostly agree that seeking spirituality as a way of avoiding physical-plane involvement and withdrawing from its lessons is rather unproductive. On the other hand, total preoccupation with the scenery and games of local circumstances involves falling entirely under the spell of what the East calls Maya—the illusion veil of the physical universe.

One cannot say that people are "wrong" for being utterly en-tranced and preoccupied with physical plane life, because a major facet of the Earth School curriculum is the exercise of free choice among the beings who are here. Free choice is probably the master teaching device of all time. Under its tutelage, everyone eventually learns their lessons well.

Michael, Orin, Mentor, Enid, and other guides have said there are no wrong choices, since any choice, including inaction, leads to eventual understanding and growth. However, there are "better" choices. If one is materially oriented to such a degree that all spiritual aspects of existence are ignored and denied, and one is willing to use any means to "win" on the physical level, this can slow one's progress and also create karmic burdens.

Expanded consciousness and increased spiritual awareness can begin to break the spell of the local circumstances and programming. It can provide a bulwark of independence against uncritical immersion in local customs and games; a personal base to view and decide from. The awakened person is also more able to actively change circumstances which are unpleasant, or that become unsuitable. Things are surely more flexible and joyful at higher vibration levels than at the lower denser ones. In these very nitty-gritty ways, the awakened are freer.

ALIENATION ON THE PHYSICAL PLANE

There is another kind of distancing from circumstances that is not at all transcendental or joyous: alienation, with its accompaniment of physical, psychological, and spiritual ill humors. According to many contemporary philosophers and social scientists, this condition has become very widespread in our world, and it is the central theme of many serious novels, movies, and plays. Man alone and adrift (for some reason, it is almost always men that are depicted), separated from his fellows, and out of phase with the world he is stranded in. Some commentators have asserted that this is the logical culmination, the end-state inherent in our left-brain Western civilization.

There is sometimes confusion among the various states of spiritual awakening and the various states of alienation. In a landmark book, *The Outsider*, by Colin Wilson, these two states are intermingled in his portrayal of the Outsider, "who sees an extra dimension." His extensive quotations from world art, philosophy, and literature make a strange mix of vaulting inspiration and abysmal despair. The major theme in all these quotations is a rejection of the world as it is.

The frequent intertwining of these two states is not accidental, because some degree of alienation, of "seeing through" the pattern of one's circumstances, is often a step on the road to spiritual awakening. People who are happy with their surroundings, or, at least, resigned to them and dutiful about carrying out their programming, don't become seekers unless something shakes them up. But people who become literally disenchanted, with their circumstances and the world in general, are potentially open to some alternatives. Without some positive alternative road, alienation by itself can be just a descent into negativism, with fewer and fewer positive experiences then available to the person. No way to live.

The evidence suggests that there is a large and growing number of people who are discontented and unfulfilled by the circumstances of our modern lives. This group may be one source of the recruits for the groundswell of the spiritual awakening movement.

The Paradigms of Culture and Spirituality

Circumstances play another important role in our story because they are the main source of people's beliefs and disbeliefs about spirituality. They are a key to understanding the bizarre present situation in which a great many people are denying, or paying little heed to, their own spiritual essences.

The widespread disavowal and rejection of spiritual manifestations in our current society is more of a puzzle than it at first appears to be. It is certainly not just a matter of evidence, of "show me." From what I can tell, there is now as much solid evidence for the existence of spiritual phenomena as there is for the effectiveness or safety of most of the new machines and substances loosed upon the public, or for most of the drugs prescribed by doctors.

How much evidence does it take?

Too little for some.

Never enough for others.

The skepticism is not really a matter of insufficient evidence, but of deeply absorbed beliefs and disbeliefs. Despite our much heralded age of empirical science, researchers have demonstrated that a person's beliefs can easily override *any* amount of evidence, and can sometimes even override direct experience.

A deep-seated focus on the physical plane is a cornerstone of most cultures, even those which have spawned major religions. The power of such a focus to bias and distort perceptions and evaluations of the cosmos has been well documented by historians and anthropologists. The eminent anthropologist, Clyde Kluckhohn, was fond of pointing out and demonstrating how Reality is always more vast than any single culture's conception of it. A great many people can see little beyond their culture's programmed beliefs. Therefore, if a culture denies or downgrades the importance of things spiritual, it should not be so surprising that most of its members will do the same. This does not mean such members are bad or wrong, but it does mean that they are less aware than they might be.

This is not enough of an explanation for the widespread denial and disbelief in a spiritual perspective in our society, however, because it oversimplifies Western culture. The West, like all modern complex societies, is not singleminded about the supernatural, nor has it ever really been. Since before the time of Plato, we have had a subterranean but strong tradition of occultism and spirituality, often suppressed but never eradicated. As one example among many, Pythagorus, one of the fathers of modern mathematics, was actually a wacked-out mystic. However, virtually all commentators agree that our prevailing beliefs are materialistic. Freud, Darwin, and many others have left us a heritage of anti-spiritual beliefs and disbeliefs in the paranormal. It is still necessary to step a bit outside conventional society and education to find real spiritual alternatives.

Now that interest in things spiritual has become so widespread, and there is more general discussion of these ideas, another factor has come into play. There is the "it doesn't compute" resistance to the unfamiliar; the same sort of future-shock resistance many people feel toward space technology and computers and widespread cohabitation among unmarried couples. It's hard to believe something that seems fantastic and that you have had no personal experience with or conscious awareness of. New Age ideas really are *new* to the majority of our population, even though they might have had some baffling personal experiences of their own. There is so much distance between these new notions about the cosmos and our mainstream conventional thinking that many people cannot jump the gap. The usual first response to a really different viewpoint is ridicule and rejection. Even avid seekers often find that they must overcome some inner resistance in order to take their next step. Whenever times change fairly rapidly, a large percentage of the population can be stranded in past patterns of thinking, doing, and believing—to no one's advantage.

Deeply ingrained cultural beliefs and resistance to the unfamiliar help explain passive disbelief in the face of the massive evidence of the paranormal and spirituality. But what about very active disbelievers who go out of their way to loudly denounce such ideas? The distinction between passive disbelief and active opposition is an important one. For example, I have a passive disbelief that there is life on the planet Pluto, but I feel no need whatever to actively campaign against the idea or to publicly denounce those who entertain it. Why do some individuals fervently oppose even the notion of the supernatural and question the sanity or honesty of anyone who believes in or even investigates it?

Our best answer to this question of zealous active denunciation comes, ironically, from studies of science and the behavior of scientists themselves. A number of recent studies, most notably those of Thomas Kuhn, have demonstrated that science is actually not nearly as neutral or as wide open to new ideas, or even as objective, as the popular stereotype of it, or the pure version presented in textbooks, would seem to indicate. Kuhn found that science actually operates on "paradigms"—systems of explicit and implicit assumptions and beliefs that become deeply rooted and are not likely to change even in the face of contrary evidence. The apprentice scientist, as a student, must learn these prevailing paradigms, be tested on them, and exhibit them, if he or she wishes to be certified. Often these "scientific" belief systems will not change much until the older generation of scientists in that field retire or die off. Note that these are not just intellectual thoughts to be easily sorted through and rearranged; they are deep seated, heavily trained-in *beliefs*, as writers from Kuhn to Seth and the Creative Visualization people have pointed out. Such beliefs usually have a strong emotional as well as mental component. To fundamentally change them, one must radically alter one's entire view of the world—not an easy task for anyone. This is why active resistance and derision are usually the first responses to a new idea. Incidentally, this is also why administrations are often so out of tune with the realities going on outside their windows, and are sometimes the last to realize that times have changed.

Spiritual experiences and ideas lie beyond the currently prevailing mainstream scientific paradigms. They contradict the conventional textbook expositions of the physical, medical, psychological, and social sciences, by which they are contemptuously dismissed, *whatever the evidence.* The really insidious part of this is that the putdowns are made with the "authority" of science and are not labelled as *opinions*, which they actually are. Such derogatory statements are often picked up by the media and then taken as truth by an uninformed and undiscerning public. In talking with people, I have been told, "Oh, my doctor says that near-death experiences are just hallucinations caused by oxygen deprivation," as if this were cosmic truth, rather than the biased, unresearched opinion it actually was.

As Dr. Helen Wambach points out in *Life Before Life*, a strictly physical explanation for mental or unusual events is almost always credited with being more "scientific". As innumerable studies have shown, people tend to strongly embrace the evidence that fits their preconceived beliefs and to dismiss the evidence that doesn't. This holds true even in the editorial choice of material for scholarly journals. I have, in my own records, cases of doctors and professionals who dismissed the paranormal with a wave of their hand and a joke. Upon close questioning, none of them had read any of the paranormal research. This is not science.

Before condemning the condemners, it is wise to remember that they have been through twenty years of intense training (programming) in physical-plane viewpoints. From such an ingrained perspective, the idea of the astral planes or of a cosmos swimming with consciousness is a lot to swallow. A surprising number of health professionals and counsellors, as well as physicists, are crossing over to a more spiritual perspective these days. But presently they are still a minority, and tend to be regarded within their own ranks as lost colleagues who have gone native, or gone astray.

For example, an eminent colleague of mine told me that Elizabeth Kubler-Ross, the grand lady of death and dying studies, has become disreputable since her New Age involvements. I thought about how Elizabeth had made thousands of friends through her helping work and that she is probably known and loved on a dozen different astral planes, but I only smiled at the remark.

There is another curious phenomenon about the force of conventional beliefs and their perpetuation. The unconventional thinking of many great men and women about the supernatural and spirituality are usually deleted in mainstream presentations of them. Conventionalized, sanitized versions of such men as Benjamin Franklin, Thomas Edison, Mark Twain, and Abraham Lincoln, that fit with the prevailing belief structure, are usually presented in the media and in schools. Their extensive nonconforming views on the occult, spirits, past lives, and so on, are edited out. Some recent writers, notably Head and Cranston, and Colin Wilson, have ferreted out much of this unconventional material and made it available to the public.

The power of belief is further demonstrated in the studies summarized by Ingo Swann, which show that believers score significantly higher on objective laboratory ESP tests than nonbelievers. In his fascinating book, *Natural ESP*, Swann also documents how our ordinary rational mind processes actually impede and interfere with the natural functioning of the paranormal faculties inherent in all human beings. He asserts that professional psychics have learned intuitively to just let the paranormal faculties operate, without any logical straitjacketing.

If beliefs have such power to fetter and distort the thinking of trained scientists, think of the power they have to shape the thoughts and feelings and actions of ordinary, untrained humans?

Direct Spiritual Experiences and Dogma

To further understand the role of circumstances, we need to make a distinction between direct spiritual *experiences* and the prevailing local doctrines or *dogmas* that are held as the accepted beliefs for explaining and interpreting the supernatural. Doctrines or dogmas about the cosmos, the nature of humanity, and the spirit (or lack of it) are a part of every society's belief structure, as Weber, Durkheim, and many other social scientists have shown. Not only are these dogmas heavily trained into the population, they are very often informally as well as formally enforced. Heretics have seldom fared well.

One of the most remarkable things about the direct spiritual experiences that have been reported, now running into the tens of thousands, is their striking similarity throughout the world, in all places and times. However, the local systems of dogma developed and promoted to explain the meaning of these cases vary almost endlessly. Take some common examples. A woman has a vivid dream in which she senses that her distant son is sick, and this turns out to be the case. Or a man, after an accident, has the clear sensation of floating above and looking down on his own body as the paramedics load it into an ambulance. There are now countless accounts of such happenings, and anyone can go out and collect more instances for as long as they wish. Except for local details, the essential stories don't vary much. However, the systems of dogma that allegedly explain these experiences have countless variations in religious, mystical, psychological, and biological premises. It is much easier to verify the truth of the stories than the validity of any of the dogmas. The two things, experiences and dogmas, are really somewhat independent of each other. One can have the experiences without embracing the dogmas, or one can believe in some dogma without having had any of the direct experiences.

There is no intention here to dismiss dogmas. We only want to look at their place in the circumstances of spirit encounters. There is no doubt at all that dogmas about things spiritual have often been of great value to human beings. They have provided comfort for a great many people in times of strife and anguish. They have reminded people that they are more than flesh. They have kept alive some concepts and ideas, however distorted, for communicating about the supernatural. They have sometimes helped show people that they were not crazy when they directly experienced spiritual incidents. In some cases, they have helped people to have such experiences. They have produced enough provocative assertions about the human condition and the cosmos to keep anybody's head churning. And, of course, they have embodied some truths about reality and the spirit, although sifting out these truths is a bit like finding some grains of gold scattered in the underbrush. You can wander for years through the religious literature of the world.

But dogmas also have a heavy down-side, as anyone who remembers being burned at the stake can tell you. *The main trouble with dogmas is that people become dogmatic about them.* This is not a light thing, because people will often oppress or even kill one another over points of doctrinal dispute. An incarnated spirit having an idea contrary to local customs can be dangerous—not to the spirit but to that incarnation.

The organized adherents of a dogma will often ruthlessly suppress and straitjacket any independent inquiry into things spiritual, branding it heresy. A catechism of dogma, taught with force, can stifle any independence of spirit, making the followers feel entirely dependent on the cant and its keepers for their salvation and spiritual growth. As if incarnate humans could really control the destinies of immortal spirits!

Zealots can, and often have, erected fossilized caste systems, with the arbiters of the prevailing dogma among those at the top levels. And, by its strictures, a dogma can hinder more than help individuals spontaneously experience their own spiritual natures. Such systems of dogma can have a political or economic focus as well as a religious one, as is the case with communism or "manifest destiny" fascism.

As Michael, Seth, Emmanuel, and many other high-level beings have pointed out, the world's major religions all began from a vaultingly high spiritual vibration level. But over the centuries, they have been distorted and interpreted by all-too-human beings with their own biases and agendas. This in no way detracts from the inspiration and comfort these doctrines have provided for multitudes of people at one time or another. And something of the spirit of the original messages usually shines through, however dimly.

But as such teachings become "humanized" over time, they come to reflect the physical-plane distortions of their keepers and editors.

And holy self-righteousness sets in. How much blood has been shed in the name of merciful Allah, Yahweh, Brahma, and the Prince of Peace? Zealots have laid waste more lives than all the criminals in the world.

Film at eleven.

Happily, there is an almost complete absence of such militancy in the spiritual awakening movement. And, happily, there have always been women and men of compassion and understanding within the ranks of all religions, who were moved by the spiritual spark within its doctrines, else probably none of us would be here.

The Suppression of Free Spirituality

Whatever the local circumstances, human societies and organizations tend to be a bit wary of free spirituality and of those who are involved with it. Established groups have a vested interest in the perpetuation of their shared physical-plane en-trancements. For this reason, they often regard traffic with the supernatural as a wild X-factor that doesn't fit in with, and might well threaten, established arrangements. As one example, anthropologists tell us that some cultures have regarded soulmate-type romantic love as a form of insanity, and were not above killing the woman involved for her bewitchings. And, from time immemorial, successful politicians have learned to publicly express the prevailing religious and spiritual beliefs as a requisite of office, whatever their private convictions were.

At the interpersonal level, many people find the possibility of psychic incidents befalling themselves or others disruptive. They don't want their business partner to get involved in some weird practice; they want the ghost in the garage to go away; they want their spiritually sensitive child to "settle down" and become a normal, healthy boy or girl. In one Eastern culture there was the belief that children who remembered the content of their past lives would die early. So a toddler could get soundly spanked for mentioning any such thing.

We live in much more tolerant times. No one is turned over to the Inquisition for mentioning that they commune with spirits or for writing a book about past-life regression therapy. Even in our very open society, however, organizations tend to screen out the paranormal as best they can. For instance, one doesn't win points in most job interviews by remarking that one has frequent out-of-body experiences. And, in most universities, one will get neither funding nor tenure for doing ESP research. Many friends and co-workers evidently warned Shirley MacLaine about the risks of going public with the details of her own spiritual odyssey.

The real impact of these circumstantial influences is demonstrated by the fact that a lot of people are still in the closet about their spiritual lives. I know personally of media celebrities and business executives and professionals of various kinds who remain fairly quiet about their spiritual interests. They are not entirely secretive, but neither are they publicly wide open. Over the years I have been warned about my own spiritual inquiries by well-meaning superiors, colleagues, and orthodox church people. And, as a capper, I received sweet offers to write two conventional textbooks instead of this book.

But times are changing, and tomorrow is not only a new day, it's a new era.

The prevailing circumstances in a particular historical place and time form a collective vibrational atmosphere that is a major part of the incarnated spirit's environment, just like the weather is a major part of one's physical surroundings. Ironically, this vibrational atmosphere is itself a psychic, that is, spiritual, phenomenon. The religious doctrines or dogmas prevailing in one's locale are a fundamental part of this atmosphere, providing some guidelines and comforts and answers, but also some possibly dangerous side-effects.

What to do? If you are at odds with your environment, you cannot easily draw strength and opportunities from it or move harmoniously within it. Most current writers on spiritual matters agree that the safest and most rewarding place from which to examine various doctrines is from a personal position of growing independence and self-awareness.

And be ready to move on. Otherwise the physical-plane lessons can be harder and more prolonged than they need to be.

Circumstances have yet another influence upon spiritual growth, or lack of it. To what extent are people encouraged by local customs to practice, to study, and to do exercises designed to facilitate spiritual awakening? If no one ever practiced riding a bicycle, we wouldn't be surprised to have a nation of non-riders. In the spiritual realms, the majority of us don't try—except under extreme conditions—which is when we sometimes succeed.

One of the most fantastic aspects of the inputs from our circumstances is that some of this input is even carried along into the Beyond, at least when we discorporate. In some respects you do take it with you.

In Earth School, the trick is evidently to learn all that is possible from our circumstances and ultimately to transcend them. The saga continues.

9

Past Lives

Are past lives for real? Most current Western science and religion says "No!" But it looks as if they may well be out-documented and out-voted before long. Both the prestigious National Opinion Research Center and the Gallup polls have been tracking public attitudes about paranormal subjects for a number of years. In 1974, about one in every seven Americans believed in the existence of previous lives. During the next decade, the figure rose to almost one in four (23%) and it has no doubt been continuing to rise. This comes to more than sixty million people in the United States alone. These statistics have surprised almost everyone. Two decades ago, there were only a few dozen therapists in the country who were practicing some form of past-life regression counselling; now there are several thousand, and several nationwide professional associations, such as the Association for Past-Life Research and Therapy, have been formed to serve them.

Current writers on the paranormal assert that everyone has frequent experiences which contain strong echoes from previous lifetimes. For instance, there is the new locale that seems hauntingly familiar or the person you'd swear you've known before (that same look, that same laugh). There is the subject you understand so easily and the "unexplainable" fear you've had all this lifetime.

Even more common than these, however, are echoes that happen almost daily but seldom reach consciousness: half-understanding the foreign dialogue in a movie; feeling stifled and short of breath in old houses; a burning sensation when someone is antagonistic toward you; an easy relationship with horses; an uneasiness around weapons or a strong fascination with them; some tingly feelings while looking at certain pictures in a history book or *National Geographic*; buoyant feelings under certain weather conditions; a strong, spontaneous physical attraction toward people with certain complexions; and so on. Such echoes are constant subliminal companions as we go about our daily lives.

People ordinarily think of reincarnation as an Eastern doctrine, but the list of great Western thinkers and artists who have also held the notion reads like something of a Who's Who In The Western World. A small sample includes the mathematicians Pythagoras, Euclid, and Leibnitz; the Greek and Roman notables Socrates, Plato, Herodotus, Cicero, Ovid, Plutarch, and Origen; the great Jewish thinker, Josephus, and the Jewish Kabbalists; the European philosophers Kant, Hegel, and Schopenhauer; the famous writers Goethe, Shelley, Keats, Balzac, Voltaire, Blake, Wordsworth, Kipling, and Sir Arthur Conan Doyle; the Emperor Napoleon; the American philosopher-writers Emerson, Thoreau, Walt Whitman, and Mark Twain; the composer Wagner; the American inventors Benjamin Franklin, Thomas Edison, and Henry Ford; the psychologists William James and Carl Jung; Lawrence of Arabia, Kahlil Gibran, General George Patton, and a good many current celebrities.

To top off this partial list, there is that world renowned nonviolent protestor who, ironically, had his spiritual awakening in the West: Gandhi. "I live in the hope that if not in this birth, in some other birth I shall be able to hug all humanity in friendly embrace".

The majority of these people claimed to have detailed memories of previous existences which they drew upon in their current lives. Much of their writings on the subject are simply beautiful, describing the human story with a vaulting grandeur, as not just a "go around once" treadmill of drudgeries and brief pleasures. Those who were contemporaries and knew one another felt they had known one another before, maybe as a "club" of older souls.

An elitist colleague of mine haughtily suggested that perhaps the more intelligent and creative among us are more capable of catching glimpses of past lives, but I think he was wrong for two reasons. First, a great many "undistinguished" people have such remembrances, or can easily be led to access them, as we shall see. Second, I suspect that if there is any such correlation, it goes the other way; that those who are somewhat open to conscious past-life influences are more likely to become noted for their wisdom and creativity as a result.

All well and good; the list is impressive, but what about some evidence. The most incontrovertible evidence and the hardest to explain away are the thousands of cases of spontaneous past-life recall by children now collected from around the world by Dr. Ian Stevenson of the University of Virginia, the internationally known psychic researcher, Memendra Banerjee, and other professional investigators. In many of these cases, the past-life details given by the children have been meticulously documented and verified. For instance, a thorough check of one child's recollections revealed that there had, indeed, been a man in the specific town who had been killed four years earlier while riding a bicycle on his way home to his wife Martha and his brown stucco home with the unusual shutters in the back room, just as the child had said.

The children are usually between the ages of two and six, and the remembrances are usually of a recent lifetime, although wisps of much earlier lives are sometimes recalled. Such detailed memories seem to fade, or at least drop from full consciousness, as the child grows older and becomes more immersed in the current life surroundings. (Some of them may have just decided to keep their mouths shut about it.)

Another investigator, Dr. Frederick Lenz, has gone around the United States collecting cases of spontaneous past-life memories among adults. Although his 127 cases came from all walks of life, there were striking similarities in their reports and striking similarities to material in the mystic tracts on reincarnation. In many cases, his subjects reported that the vivid recollections became life-changing experiences. They were triggered by such things as meeting someone they had been with before, or finding themselves in a locale they unerringly knew from previous times. For others, the trigger was through dreams or hearing music from earlier times. Most of these people had no prior acquaintance with the occult.

Dr. Helen Wambach has provided very impressive evidence for past lives by hypnotically regressing 1100 subjects and statistically analyzing the resulting data. If such reports were only fantasy, we would expect the majority to involve famous people and be "lives of destiny." But, in fact, Wambach's percentages for recollected past-life sex, race, social class, and geographic locale closely matched our best data for the distribution of these factors in earlier times. For instance, regardless of their current sex, 50.3% of the reported past lives were as males and 49.7% as females—very closely matching what we know is the human male-female birth ratio. The percent who reported lives as members of the upper, middle, and lower classes also approximated our best historical estimates for those times. Few, if any, of her subjects would have had prior knowledge of such data. I didn't. Would you?

She also found that the descriptions of the clothing worn and food habits reported by her subjects for previous lifetimes checked out against our best historical records. Again, how many people know offhand what tenth-century Mongolian women wore or ate? Not me.

Scattered throughout the reincarnation literature are documentations of the validity of a great many detailed past-life recalls. This detail often involves very obscure historical times and places, known about only by a few experts. Some examples are: the origins of the Etruscans, life in pre-Columbian Argentina, and medieval eating utensils. Any two or three of these cases might possibly be explained away as rather unlikely coincidences. But not thousands of them.

A different sort of evidence is now being accumulated by past-life therapists around the world. To put it simply, the majority of their patients get better. There are a number of different approaches used in this field, but the basic technology is fairly simple. A person comes to the therapist complaining of some phobia, or physical symptom, or unpleasant life-situation. Fairly often, the person has had no success with conventional medical or psychological treatments. Through one or another of the regression techniques, often involving some form of hypnosis, the person is led to remember and examine some past-life incidents that resonate into the present lifetime and produce the difficulty. Through such conscious examination and "discharge" of these buried incidents, the present-life condition is relieved, or at least somewhat eased. If the condition doesn't release, then recall of other incidents, usually from an even earlier lifetime, will often do the trick.

At a time when conventional psychotherapy has been falling into disrepute because of its interminable, expensive, and often fruitless performance, past-life therapies seem to have come along to rescue this profession and its clients.

The primary concern of regression therapists is, of course, to help their clients. So there is not too much emphasis on documenting the historical validity of what the clients say. But, scanning through the case histories reported by Schlotterbeck, Whitton, Sutphen, Wambach, Fiore, Paxon, and other past-life therapists, it is difficult to conceive of how the patients came up with their data by ordinary means, given their backgrounds. The data from these case histories is also consistent and dovetails with the data from NDEs, channeled spirits, and other paranormal sources. For example, the experiences immediately following body death have virtually the same core profile from all these sources. When a semi-literate truck driver reports the same experiences as medieval Tibetan monks, one can legitimately surmise that something's afoot.

"If past lives are real, why can't I remember any of mine?" is by far the most frequent question asked. Good question. What's the answer?

Actually there are several answers. The first is that a surprising percentage of people do remember at least some experiences from previous lives, enough to convince them that reincarnation is real. The real percentage is unknown because, again, the "in the closet" phenomenon is at work. I have done a fair amount of counselling involving past-life trauma. But something else has surprised me much more. Over the last twenty years, while I was conducting in-depth interviews on other subjects, I have had a number of respondents spontaneously tell me about strong impressions from previous existences that they had not told others about.

The most striking aspect of these stories, to me, was their vivid sensory content. They were not intellectual or discursive; rather, they were rich in raw sensations and emotions. For example, one man told me about the tearing pain followed by the orgasmic release of childbirth when he was a woman crossing the plains in a covered wagon, and the pleasant sensuality of nursing the baby. Another man told me how bone-wearying it was to erect the mandatory defensive Roman camp each night, after marching twenty miles in full gear as a common legionnaire. But he said there was always a feeling of arrogant pride and camaraderie that he missed today. A girl said she remembered living in the old West, how plain and "same old" the food was, how inaccurate black powder handguns actually were, and how much everybody looked forward to "get-togethers".

Several years ago, when large numbers of such reports of past-life recalls began to emerge, it was fashionable to dismiss them with the "cryptomnesia argument," which ran something like this: Alleged past-life memories are actually imaginatively constructed from buried this-lifetime memories of overheard conversations, books read, and movies seen. For instance, Uncle Ben used to come by when the person was a toddler and talk about the old West, or use German phrases. Or the child was shown a picture book about the ancient world. This kind of explanation has now been pretty much discredited by the work of Stevenson, Banerjee, Schlotterbeck and others, because there are details reported in so many of the cases that exist only in obscure records or are known only by a few experts, as we have seen. For example, only a few scholars on the whole planet know medieval Swedish or fifth-century Korean art forms.

In fact, there is an important turnaround conclusion in the findings. Although the links might not be conscious, we are drawn to certain subjects, and some early life incidents stick with us because they resonate with the contents of previous existences. Uncle Ben's German phrases stayed with the child because he or she had spoken the language lifetimes before.

Orthodox psychology is filled with assertions about how early childhood and prenatal incidents have a shaping influence upon a person's later life. This can sometimes happen. But, as Karl Schlotterbeck has pointed out in *Living Your Past Lives*, this is not the real cause. These current-life experiences only energize and give present-day form to patterns from previous lifetimes. Persons with different past-life patterns will react quite differently to similar present-life circumstances. Children from the same family are often strikingly different from each other.

The general conclusion is emerging that humans ordinarily have far more resonances with their past lives than clear conscious remembrances of them. Such resonances are the way that previous incarnations have extensive influences upon our present lives. Also, such resonances actively operate in every human being—they are universal.

These subliminal influences can be positive, such as having an easy familiarity with some subjects, or self-assurance about setting out on a new venture, or musical skills. They can also be negative, such as having a fear of travelling, or an obsession with dark-haired women with oval faces, or recurrent and medically puzzling stomach trouble. For reasons of therapeutic relief, far more attention has been paid to the negative side, but positive influences are at least as important in an individual's current and future lives.

According to many of the Eastern mystics and contemporary

channelled spirits, both the positive and negative aspects of past-life influences contribute to the evolvement of the soul. We have free choice so that we can learn the lessons of the physical plane. No lifetime, however wretched, is ever wasted, because all experience is "written on the soul." But all agree that the lessons are less painfully and more joyfully learned in the positive modes.

A second factor that contributes to the submerging of conscious past-life memories is that most of us are very much immersed in our present physical-plane lifetimes. We are very much occupied, and preoccupied, with our present web of circumstances, much like children lost within the world of an afternoon monopoly game. Research psychologists have found high correlations between the things we give our attention to, the things we consider important, and our memory for them. For example, we tend to forget the phone number of our previous residences, or of an acquaintance we're not very interested in.

There is a psychological phenomenon called "state-bound memory," which means, essentially, that memories are called forth by present situational details and circumstances closely resembling the details of an earlier incident. This documented phenomenon sheds much light on both forgetfulness of past lives and flashes of past-life memories. If I lived in Czechoslovakia several lifetimes back, few if any situations in my present life would call such memories forth. I speak, think, and do virtually nothing related to Czechoslovakia. If I spent a lifetime a couple of centuries ago as a minor English gentleman, I might have an easy, intuitive grasp of high school English lessons, and scenes of the English countryside might seem nostalgically familiar to me. (I did, and they are.) The point is that much of the specific content of past lives is irrelevant to the present.

There is a further, entirely different, factor involved in selective memory. A good many people strongly consider their Selves to be their current personality, name, and body, and they deny or feel little connection with any spiritual component. The specific identity Tommy Tucker, high school class of '55, hasn't lived before. It is the spiritual essence, the immutable "I" that lives before and again. To the degree that a person is presently low in spiritual consciousness, it inevitably follows that he or she will be low in awareness of other lives. The person who has almost entirely introverted into the physical-plane identity "Tommy Tucker," will inevitably be somewhat spiritually amnesiac and comatose regarding all paranormal phenomena. The body dies, the brain impulses fade, and the name becomes history. The *identity*, J.L. Simmons, with the thick glasses and wild hair, will certainly pass. But *I'll* be back again.

There are additional factors stacked against easy and widespread past-life recalls. Some people don't want to remember. For most people, agonizing death at the hands of torturers, coupled, perhaps, with the loss of family and possessions, is best forgotten. From regression reports, the past deaths themselves are usually euphoric releases, but the experiences of that life, and the circumstances leading up to the death, often were not so pleasant. Of course we must remember that therapists concern themselves with these very kinds of incidents. People seldom dwell upon their joys and successes and past pleasures in therapy. So the negative side is accentuated in order to relieve it.

The content of past lives also often involves former personalities that are quite divergent from our current-life identities, so they may seem psychologically remote and bizarre to us now. Furthermore, such former existences may involve aspects which are distasteful, even repulsive, to our present personalities. A world travelling pilot might have trouble recalling the dull, plodding life of a peasant. A "manly" man may resist recalling being an intimidated and submissive wife or mother. A mellow, pacifist youth might recoil from remembering being a Nazi tank commander. A prim, churchgoing matron might put up strong barriers against recollecting her former life as an easy come, easy go, tavern girl. There is a strong tendency for people to push such unacceptable memories out of sight and out of mind if faint memories do well up. As a sort of psychological safeguard, they will also tend to avoid and reject the subjects surrounding that life and the subject of past lives in general. In such a generalized tendency, the good times, the beautiful moments, and the skills of former incarnations also can get buried.

People who don't want to remember past lives are unknowingly caught in a spiritual Catch-22. Confronting past-life incidents seems too painful for them at the moment, yet such a conscious examination and "discharge" would dispel many of the negative shadows haunting them from the past. There are two answers for people in this dilemma. First, most people actually find past-life regression somewhat enjoyable and relieving. Second, any general raising of one's spiritual awareness level gives one a loftier view of past existences and abates the sting of those which were unpleasant.

We must include the prevailing cultural and religious beliefs of society as a factor that can either facilitate or repress past-life recalls. In Burma, where reincarnation is a widely held doctrine, past-life recollections and recognitions of past-life companions (and adversaries) are quite common. Do the Burmese live "better" lives? No doubt the answer is a matter of viewpoint.

All over the world, children spontaneously remember incidents from recent past lives. But in the West, and those third world countries now being westernized, the standard reaction of grownups is, "It's just your imagination." In the West, there is also a prevailing religious tradition that has officially outlawed the doctrine of past lives and has at times spent much time and effort hunting down those who embraced it. Intimidation or not, however, the belief has never died out.

There is a slightly whimsical factor that may be operating in all of this. Those humans who have achieved a high level of consciousness and spiritual awareness are also those who can most easily remember and draw upon previous lives. But, these are also the humans most likely to have transcended the wheel of rebirth and gone on to higher realms, leaving those of us who are less evolved and less remembering here. It's as if the A students are continually graduating from the physical-plane classroom. This selection factor operates to exit those who remember their past lives and to retain in our world those who don't. In this view, we'll all eventually "get there" too, but we're not there yet—because we're here.

"Please, not another life." For some people I have talked to, the possibility of past and future lives is not a glorious, transcendental notion at all—it is a gruesome idea that they don't want to contemplate. They seem unwilling, or psychologically unable, to look at the idea of doing it all again; of going through being born and growing up, of struggling to get it together and create some halfway satisfying niche for themselves in the world. They're looking for something safer, warmer, and more peaceful, even if it has to be oblivion. They don't *want* to go around more than once. One senior citizen told me repeatedly, "I just want to sleep in my wooden overcoat" (casket).

Upon further interviewing such people, I have found that many of them had seriously contemplated suicide during some period of their current life. I also found that most had gone through some periods of self-destructive behavior, such as heavy drug and alcohol use, or "who cares" debauchery. My tentative conclusion is that the weight of millenia-long karmic burdens had literally gotten them down, in the same way that a chronic illness can wear down a person's spirits and resistance. More than anything else they seemed to need a rest, which is evidently one of the main things provided for weary spirits in the Beyond.

As Barbara Clow pointed out to me, many people dislike the idea of reincarnation because it implies they *have* to come back here again to face the ecological crises and other earthly realities they may have helped to create.

To understand the position of such people more fully, we need to understand some more about karma.

10

Karma

If all of us have lived many times before, someone could still ask the question, "So what?" *Today* is when we are wrestling with our current circumstances and going for our opportunities. *Now* is when we are making it or not making it. This is true. But when we couple reincarnation with the concept of karma, our "so what" question comes alive.

In fact, it is hard to talk about previous lives without bringing in karma. Stripped of its metaphysical and religious connotations, karma might be looked at as the long-term habit patterns one has established, and the repercussions of these patterns upon oneself and others. There is a lot buried in this definition. But the most important thing to know about karma is that *it can be changed.*

These long-term patterns can be positive or negative, and they vary in a great many other ways. They basically create the life the person experiences. "As ye sow, so shall you reap, and as ye reap so shall you sow" is a part of most religious and mystical traditions. "What you put out, you get back" is a current popular version of the same idea. However, karma is a tricky concept, easily misunderstood and misapplied, and too often moralized about. This is not some sort of Cosmic Justice, handed down by a God or the Fates. Instead it is a matter of imaging and vibration levels. *What we think and do (and don't think and do) sets into motion what we experience, then and later.*

A small example might clarify all this. If you walk around and deliberately frown at the next ten people you meet, you will notice frowns on a number of their faces. If you now smile at the next ten people you meet, you will notice a significant number of smiles. This is a little bit of karma. Those who *habitually* frown or smile will encounter many frowning or smiling people. Past lives and previous this-lifetime experiences enter the picture because they have helped shape such habits.

Note well that this is not judgmental. You don't *have to* suffer through a hundred frowning people just because you frowned at a hundred people last lifetime. *You can just start smiling!* However, the habit of frowning may be pretty ingrained by now.

Karma is a cosmic and spiritual natural law inherent in the very nature of vibration levels and energy interchanges. It is also a major force in the evolution of souls. At least in the New Age versions, it has nothing to do with predestination—in fact, they are opposite concepts. Predestination says it's out of your hands; *karma says it's all in your hands.*

How easy is it to give up such predispositions? Anyone who has ever tried to quit smoking or biting their nails can tell you it's not always so easy. But millions of people *have* quit smoking and biting their nails. Millions of people have also transcended horrendous habits of violence and cruelty, or blind obedience, or feelings of unworthiness, during their evolutionary climb. To understand the "bondage" of karma and the releasing of these bonds, we need to take a closer look.

Karma is an active principle that can be broken down into several components. There are, first of all, long-term habitual responses to situations. A person who has a long history as a warrior will respond differently to situations large and small than one with a long history as a conciliator, or artist, or workaholic. Such differing manifestations will, in turn, produce qualitatively different responses from others, different environmental ambiences, and different situation outcomes. By acting "in character," each of these co-creates a world around them of comrades and adversaries, ongoing negotiated relationships and activities, craftsmanlike endeavors, or too much work to possibly get done. Note that these habitual responses have a self-fulfilling aspect to them. The warrior finds conflicts, the conciliator finds new dickerings, the artist finds new areas to apply creativity, and the workaholic finds more work.

Another component of karma is the person's belief programs, both positive and negative. Seth and the Creative Visualization people have provided us with many examples and insights about this component. The basic idea is that people successfully practice imaging or creative visualization all the time, mostly unknowingly, and mostly negatively. The physical manifestations of our beliefs then show us that they are "true." "It's going to be a headache." "I always have trouble with men." "I can never seem to get ahead." "If it ain't one thing it's another." These sorts of notions, usually unexamined and taken for granted, set us up for the experiences we then have. Through our energy broadcasts we attract situations to match our thought-forms. Much of this internal programming is absorbed from the remarks and actions of others, especially when we are vulnerable, under stressful circumstances, or in childhood. They therefore become long-term, deep-seated "positions" we hold. We also selectively perceive and remember data that fits and confirms our positions. For instance, out of fifty offhand remarks made to us, we will seize upon the three or four that confirm our position that "it's a headache" or "men are troublesome." Since our positions also have a self-fulfilling aspect, they contribute to our experiencing repetitive karmic patterns. If a person holds the belief that things really can't change, this itself is a karmic bind.

A further component of karma springs from the Like Attracts Like law. People tend to attract and associate with those of a vibration level and belief structure similar to their own. The kindred spirits then mutually reinforce each other. Associating mostly with like-minded others can keep us stuck at that level where additional similar experiences and programming accumulate, albeit with slow learning and growth. Other people of higher or lower wavelengths can sometimes reach us and lift us up or pull us further down. But the current level, and the resulting lifestyle, tends to have some inertia of its own. A rugged individualist likes and seeks out other rugged individualists who reinforce his rugged individualism, making him want to continue to be a rugged individualist. And so it goes through several incarnations. The less aware and spiritually awake we are, the less free choosing we are able to do in this process.

There is another component of karma which seems to be inherent in the spiritual evolvement process itself—soul level. This is mentioned in most of the mystic traditions and by most of the current channeled spirits. Michael, chronicled by Chelsea Quinn Yarbro, has given us a great deal of information on it. However, there seems to be very little popular awareness of the subject. The general idea is that each level—baby soul, young soul, mature soul, old soul—has its own typical character, its own challenges to overcome, its own opportunities, and its own perception and awareness levels. There is a good deal of variation among the individuals at any single level. But the nature of the level itself sets up some common boundaries and urges for all the individuals at that stage. Baby souls are timid and clumsy and hardly aware of others, so they can sometimes be unbelievably thoughtless or cruel. Young souls are the most heavily engaged in physical-plane games and goals and are sometimes zealots. Mature souls are in a struggle to master and learn from their feelings and empathies with others, and are sometimes masterful in their mundane accomplishments because of reincarnational accumulated skills. Older souls are trying to get it together as beings and to integrate the material and spiritual, and they sometimes live quiet, unassuming lives which nevertheless may touch many of those around them. Needless to say, our position in these stages has many karmic implications.

There is an interpersonal component of karma arising from our galleries of past and present-life relationships. There is continual "psychic leakage" from these other people which may subliminally reinforce some self-evaluations and positions. Also, meeting someone from a previous life can be a major event, as we will shortly see. These past-life relationships often involve unfinished business that has karmic implications for subsequent lifetimes.

Finally there is a component of karma that is collective. A mass population collectively creates its own cultural, political, and economic circumstances, which are then experienced by the individuals in that environment. This forms a part of the overarching spiritual atmosphere within which the citizens live and move. To a greater or lesser degree, all of a country's members share in experiencing the "destiny" of Israel, or Afghanistan, or the United States.

These components tend to operate together to produce a sometimes wearisome repetition of experiences. Karmic patterns can then develop over the long haul so that a person becomes set in his or her ways. One woman had a fairly successful life as a tavern maid in a ninth-century Mediterranean port city. In her next lifetime, when she became poverty stricken after her husband's desertion and she was looking around for some means to make her way, the tavern maid occupation seemed familiar and comfortable and "came easy to me." The girl ended up being a barmaid, off and on, for a thousand years.

Karmic habit configurations can sometimes become ritualized and rigid, as if they were set in concrete. We can then spend slow, arduous lifetimes merely chipping at the edges of such rigid patterns, perhaps even seeming to backslide occasionally. Our barmaid, for example, slowly learned enough about the business to eventually own her own establishment, with a corresponding increase in affluence and independence. In the process, she also slowly learned to care about other people. Both the Buddhists and the currently channeled high-level beings assure us that this kind of slow maturation leads eventually to full enlightenment and transcendence for everyone. But this slow pace is unnecessary.

In this slow "natural" evolvement process, a person will obsessively re-enact similar situations over and over, learning and growing bit by bit along the way. This is *not* a passive process. On the basis of karmic predispositions from the present and past lives, the person actively *seeks* and actively *creates* relationships and situations that fit the karmic scripts. Thus the person is an active agent, not just a historical passenger. However harsh and restrictive the circumstances may seem, there are always a continuing series of choices the person actively makes and learns from. One woman involved herself in a long string of dependent, semi-masochistic relationships over several lifetimes, until she gradually learned to assert herself and get out from under other people's thumbs. A man participated over several centuries in a long series of violent revolutions to better humanity. His summarizing of his learning experiences was interesting to me. "If you lose, it gets really grim and ugly; and if you win, you just replace one asshole leader with another."

Karmic patterns have far more force and influence when we are at a low awareness level, because we are in no condition to evaluate and step away from them. Then we simply and dumbly act them out, much like a subject obeying post-hypnotic commands. A rise in spiritual awareness, however it is brought about, is therefore crucial for changing long-term karmic positions. This is perhaps one of the deepest and most fundamental meanings of freedom.

Needless to say, people with little or no awareness of all this are stuck with tunnel vision about their own karmic patterns. They don't understand things that happen to them, and so come to believe in Fate and Luck and "whatever will be, will be" and "born under a bad sign." They may bitterly complain, "Why do these things keep happening to me?" and seek conventional explanations or labels for their situation. They may blame others, or themselves, or their genetic heritage, or the stars. They may seek consolation from a bottle, or recreational drugs and sex, or beliefs such as "life is a vale of tears." As Louise Hay says, they're doing the best they can. But it is much more useful and liberating to find out how to change our fate than to find out simply what our fate is. Who wants to be a barmaid, or a guy compelled to chase willowy brunettes, for another thousand years, anyway?

From the viewpoint of eternity, perhaps it doesn't matter how long one's soul evolvement takes. But from an in-human viewpoint, this slow development may seem a weary prospect.

Fortunately, it doesn't have to be this way. A growth in consciousness and the pursuit of a more spiritual path can break up and wash away a great deal of this karmic cement in a relatively short period of time. Nor does this have to be some astringent, self-denying process, either, because there are many adventures and delights along the way. High-spirited people are happier than low-spirited people. And they have more fun.

Todd Rundgren has a song, "Too Far Gone," that expresses the idea of having already gone too far down to turn around and climb back up. But all spiritual traditions teach that this is *never* the case.

So how can we speed up working through our karma? To what extent can therapies and consciousness-expanding programs lift our karmic burdens, altering our karmic habits and positions in the direction of improvement? To put the question another way, can our spiritual evolvement be accelerated? The answer is emphatically *yes!*

Just being *aware* of these phenomena, without doing anything else, begins to create subtle shifts in a person's psyche, so that they think, feel, and act a little bit differently, which begins to change the scripts. This is a beginning, but the process is usually not very swift.

In individual and group sessions, therapists of various persuasions have been resolving the stubborn present-life problems of clients by regressing them into past lives in which their affliction or obsession originated. Sutphen, Wambach, Schlotterbeck, Whitton, Paxon and a growing legion of others have created some remarkable alleviations of symptoms with these hypnotic and semi-hypnotic techniques. (See, for example, Dick Sutphen's very readable *Predestined Love.*) In the bargain, the client usually gains some awareness of Self as a deathless being, which can have profound after-effects, as we've seen. For example, a woman who was afraid of flying was relieved of the phobia after releasing the emotions from a past-life in which she had been thrown off a cliff. She is now an airline stewardess and New Age seminar helper. Our perennial tavern girl is now an alternative health counsellor and says she is using "a higher octave" of all her barmaid skills. Many thousands of such cases have now been documented and there is no doubt that a great many people have had their lives transformed by regression therapy.

Critics have sometimes claimed that the recalled incidents may only have been imagined. However, the evidence from Schlotterbeck, Whitton and others strongly suggests that the reverse is true: *that much of our everyday imagining springs from the subliminal content of previous lives.* Anyone who has worked much in past-life therapy can be impressed (and sometimes dismayed) by the depth and extent of a client's karmic patterns. The person may be an indentured servant or outright slave to these configurations. Resources and energies are continually stolen by these compulsions and addictions, with the only repayment being a bit of temporary pleasure or a few moment's ease.

Even more amazing, however, is the ease and swiftness with which these knots can sometimes be untangled. Even a bit of work, a couple of sessions or a weekend seminar, will often free some bonds and alleviate a chronic travail or psychosomatic symptom.

Any alleviation *always* involves at least some slight raising of consciousness. *No relief occurs without some consciousness expansion.* Overall transcendence of one's karma requires an overall consciousness raising. If you broke someone's arm in your last lifetime, you don't have to create a situation in which someone breaks your arm in this lifetime —*unless you believe you do.* If such equal and opposite paybacks couldn't be risen above, the human race would have self-destructed through mutual retributions long ago.

In addition to past-life therapies, there are a wide variety of other consciousness expansion techniques and programs to lift us out of karmic ruts and set our feet upon paths of spiritual development. These are, of course, not magic potions—we have to actively do some work.

All around the world there now are individual practitioners, groups, and institutes which help people by using some form of spiritual self-realization. There are so many of these, utilizing so many different approaches, that there is now a New Age Yellow Pages to cover them. These disciplines have a double thrust karma-wise. On the one hand, they are designed to break people loose from negative karmic habits and help them program more positive approaches in thinking and living. Simultaneously, the techniques and accompanying teachings are designed to increase the student's spiritual awareness level.

How well do they work? The nitty-gritty question. Well, they vary tremendously in approach and the practitioners also vary tremendously in level of skill. No one approach works for everyone and any approach works for some people. I suppose the simplest answer is this: Anyone who has been around the spiritual-awakening movement to any extent knows personally of dozens upon dozens of people who have been uplifted and had their lives changed through practicing some of these techniques. Sometimes the changes have been mild, sometimes awesome.

Past-life therapies and spiritual enhancement techniques are not a magic jump-start to full spiritual evolvement. They can loosen karmic bonds and help people evolve further and more quickly than they otherwise might. But, after all, they are only tools. And evolvement takes some work. The *use* of the tools is in the hands of the individual.

There is an important positive side to karma which has not yet received as much attention as it deserves. Charmed lives, assistance from other beings, easy skills, "good luck," mastery of various physical-plane activities, intuitive savvy, all may be the result of long-term positive karma one has built up. We presently enjoy and benefit directly from the spiritual evolvement we have so far achieved. Also, the Earth School lessons can be mastered more easily and swiftly. Another example of "you *can* take it with you." Barbara Hand Clow and her therapist, Gregory Paxson, in *Eye of the Centaur*, are among the few who have taken up positive aspects of karma.

Positive karma is as subtle, but as extensive and important in its influences, as negative karma. Through successive lifetimes, each being builds up accumulating personal and interpersonal resources. Like compounding interest, we can then further build upon the accumulation until we are rich in the truest meaning of the word.

Mature souls, because of their extensive experiences, can usually master physical-plane endeavors rather easily. Although they have other challenges to surmount, school (which is partly re-education) usually comes easily to them. Old souls can do just about anything they want, from achieving acclaim to being astonishingly successful wastrels, although they often choose simple lives. Even in these simple lives, they easily manage to arrange their comforts. They too have their challenges, but they are hardly at all vulnerable on the mundane level.

Think of the positive karma that someone like Saint Francis has accumulated by now, with friendships and assistance awaiting him from beings on a thousand different worlds. Think of the music that Mozart must be creating by now. Think of the things you do that are really rather miraculous when you step back and take a psychic look.

None of us would be physically alive today without massive support from our own accumulated positive karma.

11

Past-Life Relationships

If tomorrow your romantic partner or child had a different hair color and a different physical body, could you recognize him or her among a dozen people?

Astronomers tell us that each star has its own unique "signature," its own profile of characteristics and qualities that set it apart from any other star. There are classifications of stars to be sure, but the stars in any class share only some similarities; no two are ever identical. In the same way, each soul has its own signature, like no other soul. At some subliminal level, souls display the ability to *recognize* one another. This recognizing can occur however the fleshly envelope looks, whatever the surface personality is, and whatever the physical-plane circumstances are. Meeting someone who seems inexplicably *familiar* is one of the most real and commonly reported paranormal experiences of all.

Such unaccountable familiarity has its roots in shared previous lifetimes, although in the Western world it is usually not recognized as such. However, the feelings in such a case can be very strong, and other people can seem like strangers by comparison. Ironically, this is presently often referred to as "chemistry," although chemistry has nothing to do with it.

The shared past experiences can be extensive, covering long periods of time, or intensive, involving highly emotional incidents, or both. Also, they can be highly pleasant, mild, or rather unpleasant. Whatever the past content was, good or bad, the present contact can cause the welling up of strong emotions and body sensations. These age-old connections mean that nothing could be further from the truth than "love at first sight." Thus, besides "love at first sight," there is "fear at first sight" (a former executioner), "gentle warmth at first sight" (as toward a former child or favored pupil), "merriment at first sight" (a former wild youthful companion), "hate at first sight" (a former oppressor), "deep friendship at first sight" (former comrade-in-arms), "comfort at first sight" (former good acquaintance), and so on. If the previous-life relationship involved heavy loss or unfinished business, there may well be a psychological clutching toward the other person, an "I don't want to lose you (again)" desperation. Even without this, the current meeting is likely to have a haunting quality to it because of the leakage of other memories from that time.

Positive sorts of karmic connections from previous lifetimes have received much attention in the writings of Edgar Cayce, Jess Stearn, Dick Sutphen, and the reincarnationists in general. The "soulmate" is the most intense of these, in which affinities between two spirits are so great that they can achieve the extreme of togetherness, partially melting into one. The two beings, if they find one another, will literally do anything to be together, the magnetism is so strong. And if separated they are stricken, sometimes mortally. The soulmate experience is overwhelming and can sweep everything else away—current family, career, whatever. Some claim we have only one soulmate, some say several, and some say that far up the spiritual evolutionary line *everyone* becomes a soulmate.

Past-life therapists have written most about the more negative kinds of karmic relationships: ancient fears, dreads, and hatreds which color the current lifetime. Spontaneous discomfort or dislike on meeting someone seem at least as common as spontaneous liking or love. These seem to always involve some unresolved conflict or spiritual indebtedness, and seem best thought of as unfinished business, or what Michael refers to as the burning of karmic ribbons. Although concrete actions may sometimes be required to balance the books, the resolution of such long-term conflicts seems mainly to require infusing the connection with understanding, compassion, and acceptance of responsibility for one's own actions in the matter.

The vast majority of karmic relationships are too complex to be placed simply in plus or minus categories. For example, I counselled one pair who had been together for at least a dozen lifetimes, mostly as companions but sometimes as lovers, and once as parent and child. The shared emotions included good times, precious moments, sexual thrills, griefs, betrayals, falling outs, infidelities, aid and emotional support, bereavements, and boredom, not to mention going broke together and getting rained on together. Not surprisingly, their feelings toward one another were deep but complicated. As they continue to evolve, the spiritual guides tell us that these intricacies will be washed away, leaving between them only a love "that passeth understanding."

During previous lifetimes, people have, at one time or another, made solemn vows, often under stressful conditions. "We'll be friends forever." "I'll get even with you." "We'll meet again." "Lovers 'til the end of time." "I'll never forget you." And, in a very real karmic sense, they don't forget.

Meeting someone known in a past life, even when there is only a dimly felt resonance, can upset the established lives and relationships of the parties involved. This is especially true for those who have little or no conscious awareness of spirituality or reincarnation. Objectively, just because someone was your lover or executioner a couple of hundred years ago doesn't mean you must sleep with them or fear and attack them now. But, subjectively, the compulsion to do so might overwhelmingly influence you to continue the past drama.

Running into someone from a past life, although perhaps electrifying, can therefore be something of a mixed blessing. It can mean trouble. If there is unfinished business or an unresolved conflict from the former relationship, there may arise an overwhelming urge to just pick up where things left off long ago. This may produce bizarre behaviors in the present time. The more buried away from consciousness the past memories are, the less able the person is to distinguish between "then" and "now."

How widespread are these phenomena and how frequently do

they happen in most people's lives? At this point, we don't really know. But our emerging paranormal picture suggests that these subliminal pushes and pulls—toward one thing and away from another—may often mark the milestones in our lives and are significant factors in our relationships.

For all of the possible problems, contacts with people known in previous lives should not be thought of negatively. They can be a bounding joy, a spiritual re-energizer; they can be psychologically uplifting. The behavior that results may seem outlandish to some, but this is a matter of viewpoint. Sometimes some outlandishness is just what an individual needs to kick free of the treadmill he or she has gotten onto.

Even when there is some pain and inconvenience involved, it is better in the long run to open up to past lives and spiritual awareness in general. These things affect us anyway, whether we are conscious of them or not. If we are conscious of such influences, we can be more in control of our destinies.

Recall of past lives can be fine if we remember that *then was then and now is now.*

One of the greatest benefits of a reincarnation perspective can be a significant lightening-up of feelings about present-life circumstances and the subjects of life and death in general. We know we will have other chances, other games to play, other careers, and other loves. So we don't have to cling so desperately to what we have now. Losses are still real and still hurt, but they don't have the overwhelming sting of a "never again," one-life perspective. Growing older physically isn't such a melancholy thing. We can play the game of life with a lighter heart when we know that, whatever happens, there will be other chances.

A subject that is perhaps more important than past lives is *future lives*. When people first get interested in reincarnation, they often become entranced with who and where they have been in previous historical times. This is understandable, and maybe a necessary focus to center themselves and drain off some of the trauma of some episodes. But the current lifetime is where the action is. And what about the future?

That we will live again and again is inevitable, it would seem. *How* we will live in the future, and what shape we will be in, is not. If it is true that we've made our bed in the past, then it is true that we are making our bed for the future. In plainer language, the futures we experience are largely in our own hands. The choices we make in the present create our future reality. If we just leave future lives (and the rest of this one) in the hands of "fate," we actually are just passively leaving it all in the hands of our karmic habit patterns. "As ye sow, so shall you reap" turns out not to be a moral judgment, but the statement of a cosmic natural law.

As we grow in awareness, we can often see a good deal of our karmic patterns and the effects they produce. From this higher vantage point, we often can change some aspects of the pattern through simple recognition, Creative Visualization, or similar techniques. In doing so, we literally change our immediate and long-term future. We can replace habits with purposes, and compulsions with conscious intentions. This isn't necessarily an easy process; but even a bit of success can make a significant difference. By changing just one strand, we change the weave.

From this higher vantage point, we can also see some of the strands that intertwine us with other beings. One question sometimes asked is, with the multitudes of people on the planet, how is it we run into so many people known in former lifetimes? Wouldn't the laws of chance lead to this happening only rarely? Yes—but such karmic connections are not a matter of chance at all. For one thing, the Like Attracts Like principle is operating; karmically bonded people are to some degree drawn to similar places and circumstances. Also, there are subconscious affinity channels that create subtle converging vectors, increasing the likelihood of a meeting. There is evidence, from past-life regressions gathered by Wambach, Whitton and others, that many such connections are planned for prior to birth. There is the fact that the other person is, at some level, questing too, which increases the odds of getting together. Finally, we may screen through hundreds, even thousands, of acquaintances before a connection is recognized. All of these factors increase the odds of connecting. But still, connections are often not made and must wait until some future lifetime. For example, some people I've talked to feel that they will find a soulmate in some future lifetime, and have an impressive amount of patience about the waiting.

With an acceptance of reincarnation and spiritual evolution, we can take a longer view of things. This can be at the personal, the interpersonal, and the world level. At the personal and interpersonal levels, we might wish to introduce some changes to avoid going through the same scenarios again. At the world level, it might seem wise to take some responsibility for the environment, the populace, and national and planetary circumstances in general. We will return to breathe in the air we are now breathing out, and to live within the conditions we are now collectively setting up. Environmentally speaking, today's garbage is tomorrow's soup.

The idea of past lives has implications that may be extremely uncomfortable for some. We don't all have the same experience patterns, far from it. But the fact that we've all lived so many lives under so many different conditions means that, at some time or another, we have all done just about everything, and had just about everything done to us. So no one is really in much of a position to cast the first stone. In this sense, none of us are very innocent. There are no virgins here.

There is a more positive way to look at this. We are all comrades on the journey and companions on the road.

"Out of sight" and "out of mind" certainly do not mean without influence, when it comes to past lives. The more repressed and "forgotten" they are, the more their influence is out of our control. So their subtle and not so subtle echoes are worth becoming sensitive to.

Knowing about past lives doesn't vanish today's toothache or erase all grief over the loss of a loved one. It doesn't necessarily lower your monthly bills. You may still have to call the plumber when your sink gets stopped up and it may not make things go smoother with the next person you meet. But it can change the way you think and feel and act. And that will end up changing everything else. It surely puts a different perspective on things.

12

Sex & Spirituality

Human beings have been somewhat preoccupied with sex since time immemorial. And societies have usually woven elaborate rules and rituals around the sexual activities of their members. Sex is sometimes a source of intense pleasure and sometimes an avenue for establishing an intimate bonding between beings. It is also sometimes a source of deep turmoil and feelings of guilt, shame, failure and suicidal depression. For some people, sex is a form of recreation, for others it is an addiction. For some it is a duty, mildly pleasant or somewhat odious. And some people have found it easier to just turn their backs on the whole subject for awhile in their evolutionary journey. But what about sex and spirituality?

Since the spirit is involved with every aspect of living, it should not be surprising that it is involved in many different ways with sex. We've already seen that sexual attractions can be based on karmic habit patterns or shared past-life experiences. Interpersonal psychic influences can also involve sexual energy vibrations and subtle erotic extra-sensory interchanges. The soul, in its current stage of evolvement, will also have certain points of view with regard to sex. And disembodied spirits often involve themselves in sexual matters.

To better understand the relationships between spirit and sexuality, we must focus on sex, not love and romance. There are links between sex and love, but fewer than many people think, and fewer than popular music and novels suggest. Sex, love, and marriage are often three different subjects, as any errant knight will tell you. Sometimes they are combined, and this can be very satisfying if both parties are in accord, but they are really separate topics.

Regarding sex, there is a sort of scale of descending coarseness of vibration level, or you could also say, a scale of ascending refinement of wavelength of thoughts, feelings, and behavior. On this scale there seem to be four different bands of sexuality from "low" to "high," each shading into the adjacent levels. The spiritual law of Like Attracts Like certainly holds sway here, although it is modified by body-type attractions and local circumstances. This scale seems to hold true for in-humans and disembodied spirits alike; it seems to exist on both the physical and astral planes. (For those readers who are interested, there is a correspondence between these levels and the predominance of the various chakras or energy centers of the spirit-mind-body configuration.)

Level One, the lowest band, could be termed *addictive sexuality*. It has been described with words such as lust, debauchery, and pornography, although none of these really captures the raw realities of this level. Some of its elements are promiscuity, an abandonment to sensation, an attitude of "anything goes," a seeking of hot ultimate wickedness, a surrender to body heat. These activities are frequently accompanied by the heavy use of liquor and drugs. Level One is essentially the profile of an addiction.

Like drug addiction, this habit dominates the person and there is a cyclic insatiability. Frequently there is also a longer term sequence: can't get enough, more and more stimuli needed for the turn-on, seeking the ultimate orgasmic high and release, and eventual burn-out. The physical body can get pushed beyond its limits if one is pursuing this level's activities, so chronic low-grade illness is common in this band. Level One addictions also tend to draw in disembodied spirits of the low astral wavelengths.

A portion of modern populations go through a phase of this at some period in their lives and a much smaller proportion inhabit the band chronically. Others go through it vicariously in an autoerotic fantasy life, sometimes in unknowing subliminal partnership with less evolved earthbound spirits. For example, many of the fantasy companions imagined by individuals during masturbation are actually manifestations of real spirits. Those who have gone through a Level One phase (and survived) speak eloquently about how it was a sort of madness, a walk on the wild side. It has the attraction of crazy self-abandonment. What they describe is a dependency, a "don't care anymore" escapism from some circumstance, a craving for the thrill of release. Like a bring-down after drug use, there is usually a depressed, empty feeling afterwards, relieved only by more of the same. There is frequent suffering from psychosomatic ills, plus real bodily deprivations resulting from the lifestyle. And sometimes little memory of the partying: "You can only tell how good a time you had by checking to see how bad you need a shower."

Just as a society can be programmed to hanker after the "glories of war," so a populace can be programmed by the media and mass thought-forms to yearn for the thrills of hot sex and the swinger's world. In both cases, one might do well to check out the real scene before signing up.

At this level the psychically strongest persons may attract a cluster of others, whom they then dominate and abuse. In doing field research, I have run into many of these little groupings in a wide variety of circumstances, and in just about every walk of life. Level One people will also often degrade others with some help from low astral beings that hang around singles bars, hotsheet motels, and restrooms. The seduction offered is the thrill of the downhill slide.

This level is a feeding ground for less evolved disembodied spirits who hover around the orgy and feed upon its vibrations, images, and sensations in a rather ghoulish manner. If drugs are involved, they will often further open up connections with the psychic realms, pulling in more low-level astral beings.

There is a kind of shared outlook and camaraderie at this level, but betrayals, because of impulse or expediency, are routine. Life at this level does have a perverse intensity, but it is stark and unstable; and it is dangerous physically, psychologically, and spiritually. Paranormal beliefs at this level are likely to be in such things as dime-store astrology,

Ouija boards, fortune telling, fate, luck and signs, also some fiddling with darkside magic spells and potions. Level One can be an addiction which ties a being to an obsessive physical-plane focus. It is understandable that those who come out of it often display the "reformed whore syndrome." It is almost certain that we all go through this at some time in our Earth School adventures. And we survive it and learn from it. Seth did. Buddha did.

Level Two might be termed *healthy eroticism*. This is the province of those who identify strongly with the physical plane and their bodies, but in a nonpathological way. Level Two is *physiological*; healthy, satisfying sex, like a hearty meal after a day's labor. There is a sort of biological compliance with the breeding urges of the body.

Here people have identified very strongly with the physical side of their nature. Friends and family often encourage this pattern: a healthy young couple should settle down, marry, and breed the next generation. Level Twos tend to be especially concerned with (and hung up on) body appearance, their own and others, which can be a heavy constraint on interpersonal relationships. They tend to judge other humans largely in terms of physical appearance and don't even like to be seen with the disfigured, or those who diverge from what is locally considered fashionable in physical attractiveness. As many have eventually discovered, however, "good looks" are no guarantee whatsoever of a mutually satisfying relationship. The divorce courts are full of pretty people.

Level Two is called healthy, but this is a narrow physical-plane view of the matter. It may be satisfying at the mundane level but it is literally lacking in spirit. I'll wager that your dog, the last time it was in heat, didn't craft a candlelight dinner, or come up with some poetry, or care about its partner as much as itself. At this level, others tend to be viewed as objects to somehow be snared and possessed. Level Two is, however, often a relatively stable place from which to start one's growth and maturation. Many couples who began their relationship at Level Two have gone on to higher levels as their relationship deepened.

Level Three might be termed sweet *sensuality*. This is the band of romantic love songs, sweet kisses, and sweet dreams. Surrenders. Magic moments. At this level, considerations about physical appearance are often overriden by personal qualities and resonances between the two beings. Psychic experiences are sporadic but real, and the persons involved are often at least semi-aware of them. The relationship is something of an artistic collaboration with higher level spiritual overtones. This is a finer vibrational level. The participants find Level Two drab and uninteresting and are turned off by Level One. There is an aversion to pornography, not on moral grounds, but because of the wide divergence between the two wavelengths. To those at Level Three, moments of sharing, and playful interactions, may be as memorable as physical lovemaking.

Many people make something of a career of Level Three relationships, devoting a great deal of their energy and focus to them and deriving the majority of their pleasures and satisfactions from them. A lot of fairly direct spiritual contact with other humans can occur at this level and this can be exhilarating. If a particular relationship turns sour, these people are crestfallen, but they tend to soon go on to establish another one. Such relationships, and the experiences surrounding them, often provide a good deal of personal and spiritual growth.

Those who are manifesting Level Three wavelengths, but who are sexually lonely and frustrated, are not infrequently visited sensually during sleep states by discarnate spirits who enjoy these vibrations, and who are sometimes companions of the person. Such "dreams"—often only half-remembered—can be haunting.

What would have happened if Romeo and Juliet had lived, married, and had children? The idea deserves a sequel to the original play. Often, we are never told the aftermath of the Level Three passions expressed in literature and song. Such relationships can be meaningful without being enduring. It is rigid moralism to assert that a couple should stay together when the relationship is no longer working. But even in our day of somewhat easy sexuality and the frequent changing of partners, many Level Three people still reach a deep abiding level of physical and spiritual bonding.

Level Three often represents a fine balance between spirit and body, each enhancing the other through a sexual relationship. Such a balance, as it is experienced sometimes, provides the platform for growth into Level Four.

Level Four, the highest, can only properly be called *transcendent*, because it does, indeed, seem to transcend space and time and everything else. Considerations of time, place, station in life, and circumstance can be swept away by its fervor. Magic moments transmute into mystical experiences and, for those involved, the rest of experience may pale into insignificance. The persons are attuned to each other even over physical distances, and ESP with some direct awareness is very common. Intimacies are more than sexual/physical, because of the high level of psychic energy interchanges between the participants. Basically you have two spirits in a relationship, with their bodies as vehicles. The words "companion spirits" and "soulmates" are sometimes used in referring to this level. Persons who have gotten stuck in negativity might say this is too good to be true, and, if true, it is almost too good for this world. How high up does this level go? Perhaps one could say, "God only knows."

People have been known to walk away from dazzling careers, happy families, even kingdoms, for the sake of transcendent sexual connections. So society is somewhat ambivalent about them. On the one hand, all the world loves a lover, but on the other hand it is sensed that these pairings can upset anything (and everyone). Much of the world's great literature and music deals with this theme, but unfortunately, usually in a tragic vein.

If the lovers are parted by physical-plane circumstances, there is often the intuitive knowledge that they will be together again under different and more benign conditions. ("There's a place for us.") The link is considered immortal, and there's growing New Age evidence that in fact this can be the case—that such spiritual contact is never really lost. The pull of such a liaison is almost irresistible and the affinities between the beings are deathless. So death is no barrier.

The spiritual involvement at Levels Three and Four lends a great deal of the euphoria and ecstasy to ordinary romantic affairs. To say that this is "chemistry" is a grave reversal of the truth.

Note the changing roles of spirit and body as one ascends the levels. In lust and pornography, the body has the day and the spirit is hardly evident. Near the top level, the spirit is virtually, but probably never completely, in full sway, with the body an instrument to be played upon.

Aftermaths vary with the levels, too. Activities on Level One often produce a dissolute, "grey ashes" sort of feeling afterwards. Level Two commonly produces a sort of animal satiation, similar to the successful handling of any body function. Level Three engenders a lingering sensuality, a languid warmth and fulfillment. In a sense there is no aftermath at Level Four, because of its timeless quality. But physical-plane distractions, the call of duties and commitments and other tasks, mark the end point of the specific sexual activities.

At Level One there is a good deal of enforced sex, including rapes, sexual payoffs for favors, and sado-masochistic partnerships. At Level Two there is expected sex as part of the routines of living. At Level Three and Level Four, sex is part of the interpersonal dance, and one can legitimately speak of "making love" as opposed to "having sex." Those who are more spiritually evolved and aware have little interest in enforced sex of any kind, because they have empathic awareness of the sensations and emotions of their partners — an empathy which also makes them better lovers.

As with other areas of living, Like Attracts Like, so each of these levels attracts vibrations of its own kind. Also, each level tends to attract discarnate beings of similar wavelength, who may involve themselves in the couple's activities, both sexual and otherwise. More evolved beings are not much interested in voyeurism; they've been through it all, or have transcended it in some other manner. But lower level ones sometimes thrill to and thrive on it. More evolved beings seem to encourage, augment, and take "contact high" pleasure in the warm, sharing emotions of sexual activities at Levels Three and Four. Perhaps all the living cosmos loves a lover. Truth to tell, there may well be no such thing as entirely private or solitary sex.

The law of attraction also influences what level of being will inhabit the child when a pregnancy occurs. Low astral and earthbound spirits will sometimes be attracted to Level One activities and get pulled into incarnating in the resulting infant. Woe unto the disembodied being drawn into a Level One pregnancy. Level Ones tend to alternate brutality and neglect with smothering sentimentality. Level Twos produce what is sometimes disparagingly called "peasant stock." The child is likely to be treated fairly well and trained in the ways of the prevailing local circumstances, although the child's psychic sensitivities are likely to be forcibly dismissed as unwholesome imaginings. Level Threes and Fours tend to provide a more multidimensional environment for the child, and less rigid programming, so that his or her natural predispositions can more easily flower.

Intensity and passion exist on all of these levels; the difference is in how they are manifested. Those stuck at lower levels will sometimes sneer at upper level persons and activities as square and naive. This happens because such "precious moments" as holding hands for a second, or touching one another's hair, or an exchange of understanding smiles, are often too subtle for lower vibration level individuals to perceive. The joke and the loss is on them however, since they are hearing only the base notes of the music.

However, it seems that the yearning for more spirituality is never entirely absent, because persons in the lower bands often express the yearning for a higher love. In the desultory aftermath of partying, a woman may think wistfully about finding "a nice guy," and the athlete or musician, after a post-performance orgy, wonders if he'll ever find a sweet companion to really share his world. Housewives stuck in a Level Two routine may long for a sharing, understanding, sensuous relationship. Meanwhile their husbands are daydreaming about nurturing liaisons in which they would be accepted as themselves and maybe find some shelter from the storm.

There are, of course, contacts and movements between the levels. Level Twos, in youth or during conventions, will sometimes have a fling on Level One, but afterwards will usually look down contemptuously on their partners. Level Threes will sometimes stumble into lower level involvements, but they usually find the experiences distasteful and end them quickly. People at lower levels will frequently go through a series of affairs looking for "something more," and be disappointed when they find nothing new. They will then often blame their luck on the supposed nature of the opposite sex, never realizing that we script our own lives, and that the relationships they seek are simply not possible at coarser vibration levels.

Sometimes lower band people do succeed in finding higher level relationships, with some active assistance from the higher level partner. But for these to be stable, the lower karmic positions must be overcome or erased. This can be done. I've personally seen many people do it through some consciousness-expansion experience or program. Luckily for all of us, there are contagions of upliftment as well as contagions of degradation and negativism.

When we observe people over several lifetimes, we can readily see that *everyone* has occupied all the lower bands. Evidently we must go through all of these levels as part of our all-around experience on the physical plane. So it would be foolish to arrogantly condemn those going through lower level phases, if we happen to be currently on a higher wavelength. We each follow our own path, and getting up to higher levels will occur naturally with further evolvement.

It is too easy to moralize about these levels, because in-humans have such strong morally and emotionally programmed beliefs about sex. In our allegedly more enlightened times, many people still become needlessly hung up about who they have slept with or what their current desires are. Chronic guilt and shame are unnecessary, self-inflicted maladies. Let it go. And let go of blaming anyone else.

Like any area of human living, sex can be abused, but people are not tainted by their past sexual activities, except by their own beliefs. Underneath it all, there seem to be only two fundamental problems with sex when we strip away the local moral customs. One: it can become addictive and can therefore prolong one's sojourn on the physical plane and slow one's evolution. Two: because it can be addictive, individuals sometimes spiritually abuse others for the sake of sex.

Sexual repression of oneself or others solves nothing in the long run either. The repressed images, emotions, and desires will just come out in some other area, or later in some more virulent form. Turning one's back on the whole subject is all right as long as one realizes that one will have to pick it up at some later time. On the physical-plane segment of our evolvement, it seems that withdrawal, even though it's sometimes necessary or wise, really only means deferment.

You might think this is about all there is to the subject except for the wet and wonderful details. But physical sex is only the beginning.

There is the astral sex engaged in fairly frequently by incarnate humans while they are in a sleep or trance state. These sensual visitations and meetings occur between those with vibrational resonances (Like Attracts Like again) and are described by many writers as more enthralling and satisfying than their strictly physical counterparts. There is much evidence that lovers who are physically separated often do this subliminally, but have little recognition of the shared experiences in the waking light of day. These avenues can also be a haven for the lonely, who cannot find what they are looking for in their physical surroundings. Since thoughts and intentions are manifested directly on the astral levels, those with unfashionable bodies can clothe themselves in any form, beauteous or otherwise, that they desire.

It turns out that adepts have been messing around with these forms of astral sexuality for millenia. This is a not much advertised aspect of underground mystic traditions throughout the world. A growing number of people are now learning to do this in a conscious, somewhat controlled manner through the wide dissemination of information about out-of-body and astral techniques once available only to those initiated into the inner circles of esoteric schools. Such techniques are laid out, for example, in Gavin and Yvonne Frost's book, *Astral Travel*, which has a refreshing pagan quality. These techniques have many purposes and capabilities in addition to out-of-body sex. Most people, after the first flush of such experience, turn more and more to other matters, such as exploring the astral levels and communicating with their inhabitants. On their own, most initiates soon realize that obsession with astral sensuality can stall their evolvement. They also come to sense that there are much "better" and more joyous experiences available further up the line.

Moving on to disembodied spirits, there are some continuous group sex orgies in some of the lowest levels of the astral realms. A spirit can either consciously or compulsively manifest any ethereal form. Some who are stuck in obsessive sexual passions attempt to work them out in these astral-realm "human sexual piles," as Robert Monroe calls them. The vibrational wavelength is evidently our Level One, but without the limitations of physical-plane bodies with their exhaustions and other needs. Before anyone gets too eager at this prospect, however, know that all those who have viewed it have reported on the overwhelming waves of frustration and sadness emanating from these piles of writhing forms. The scene produces shudders rather than turn-ons among the viewers. By all accounts, this is no place to get stuck for an eon. In this range there are also the earthbound spirits who hover around copulating couples at the lower wavelengths. A singles dance bar is crowded, indeed. Only part of the haze is tobacco smoke.

Above these ranges, other activities come into play. In the mid-astral levels, sexuality seems to be a kinetic discharge and sharing of energies, like the mingling of fields between two electrical poles. This is a sort of rushing together and simultaneous consummating release of unbalanced energies. The surrender to the experience is entirely voluntary and mutually consenting. In-human equivalents of this might be the first thrills and ardor between new lovers, honeymoon passions, and hot one-night-stands that later fade away.

Those who have practiced this claim it is more fulfilling than physical-body sex, and there is no post-coital letdown. Any abuses or use of force are simply impossible at this level. Because of its very nature, this experience can only occur between consenting and desirous partners. Grandmother was really not so foolish in wanting to hug you. I'm convinced that physical touching among humans is a weak version of the same process. Go hug a couple of willing people and see if you don't feel better.

Above these levels, on the higher astral planes, occurs something that all these other sexual practices are evidently an incomplete, partial form of. When they have evolved sufficiently and are "ready," individual spirits completely meld into one another, sharing all of their energies and experiences and becoming one "larger" spirit. This is not just closeness or togetherness. This is complete union, a simultaneous, total, mutual surrender and possession. The spirits thus united then go on to completely meld with other spirits, in a continually expanding communion. In the act of sharing all memories, feelings, experiences and viewpoints, there is an explosive expansion of consciousness for each of the individual spirits involved. Talk about consummating a relationship!

In such melding together, the individual soul never loses its own self-awareness or independence of consciousness. It's all gain and no loss.

Talk about sharing! The composite entity has all the past experience and knowledge from its component consciousnesses available. Any of this can be *fully* re-experienced. There is also a total amalgamation of male and female, yin and yang energies. The entity is androgynous. Such melding would seem to require a degree of openness and lack of egocentrism that is hard for us to even imagine while we are still focused on the physical plane. Among humans, the high one-for-all-and-all-for-one camaraderie of some groups, or the intense sharing between bosom buddies and lovers, may be rudimentary foretastes of such spiritual unions. Also, the haunting, yearning quality of searches for soulmates may be a dim recognition of our evolutionary direction. It certainly seems to be the ultimate antidote to loneliness and that hollow feeling of separateness that most of us know too well.

13

Spirit, Mind, Body, Environment

While incarnated on the physical plane, a human being lives his or her life course within the intersection of spirit, mind, body, and environment. This fact has many interesting and important implications and it also can generate a good deal of confusion for the individual. What gets really complicated and fascinating is the interplay among these four elements. Each one influences all the others in "good" or "bad" ways which create both problems and opportunities. These mutual influences are not straight-line cause and effect (X causes Y and Y causes Z). Rather they are what scientists call an "Interaction Model," in which each component simultaneously influences all the others which are, in turn, influencing it.

In recent years, a good many professional people in the human potential and spiritual awakening movements have been studying the intertwinings of these four factors. They have found many implications of this Interaction Model. For instance, you can make someone feel better physically by cheering them up or you can make someone more cheerful by helping them feel better physically. We now know that a distressed mind can produce illnesses and a stressful environment can distress the mind. And a significant degree of spiritual awakening can change it all. But the mind can block or ignore promptings from the spirit. Meanwhile, the body is healing itself all the time—otherwise none of us would be physically alive.

If a person wants to get well, almost any treatment will work; if they don't, nothing will. Some people have walked away from a dozen bullet wounds; others have gotten a chill from an open window and died.

The spirit is the senior element in this configuration, but, as we've seen, it is neither omniscient nor omnipotent and is itself in the process of evolving. It is the "essence" of the person that is developing through its experiences of incarnating on the physical plane in a series of human bodies. Minds, bodies, and environments provide the tools and raw materials for this process. Those who are utterly entranced by the physical plane believe that the physical universe will exist long after they have gone, but the reverse is true; we will still exist long after the physical universe has vanished.

The mind seems to be best described as a marvelous programmable computer which interfaces with the spirit on one side and the body on the other. But this is only an analogy. At the very least this mind-computer is far advanced beyond anything we currently have from science. It has layers, capabilities, and mysteries that make the analogy very suspect.

The most important point about the mind, whatever it is, is that it is programmable—by circumstances, by others, by past karmic habit patterns, and by oneself. A great many people have a capricious and accidentally programmed computer running their lives. Jose Silva likes to say that the untrained mind is like a drunken monkey lurching from thought to thought.

The mind is not the physical brain, although it utilizes the brain for many of its functions. Nor is it the person's consciousness, although consciousness is in intimate partnership with the mind. People have some intuitive awareness that they are not identical with their minds. This awareness is expressed in such common sayings as, "I'm improving my mind," or "I'm going out of my mind," or (perhaps the truest of all) "I've made up my mind."

Among such sayings, the one that is hottest for the spiritual awakening movement is: "I've changed my mind." Change your mind and you change your future.

The body is a sophisticated biological vehicle for the person to occupy during physical incarnations. It has its own wisdoms and cellular awareness. It has a lot of work to do and it deserves thanks and appreciation like any good host or hostess.

The body is one's anchor to the mundane level of existence. It is also our "legal" address. Our relationships, both impersonal and intimate, exist legally on the basis of the body, even though they ultimately rest on the creations of the spirit and mind. When bodies are pronounced dead, that, in most senses, is the end of the marriage, the friendship, the business contract, at least as a physical plane reality. The spirits involved can maintain their ties, and often do, but society's legal arrangements are based on bodies.

In Western (and westernizing) societies, people identify most strongly with their bodies. In fact, many people strongly believe they are *only* their bodies and that even the mind is only some sort of subjective froth resulting from biochemical actions. They also identify and respond to others only as bodies. Ironically, however, they will sometimes complain bitterly when others see them only as bodies, for instance as sex objects or labor hands, used and exploited by others. In the West we tend to feel closer to our bodies and more distant from ourselves as spirits.

The environment is the set of circumstances within which we conduct a life while occupying a biological body. It is made up of what scientists call "contextual variables," the atmospheres within which we live. Like any atmosphere, these influence but don't determine what a person does. They are a collective co-creation of the beings involved, and they set the stage for the quality of life the person experiences. The environment sets up both barriers and opportunity channels for what is easy, possible, unlikely, and impossible in current physical-plane activities. Through its inputs, the environment also programs our belief structures to a fair degree. We often then act out this programming in a self-fulfilling way, as Seth and the Creative Visualization people have pointed out.

Because of their deep and extensive programming, the environment is the component most unexamined and taken for granted by the majority of people. They may quibble over who should be president or where to build a dam, but the broad outlines of the environment are just thought of as "the way things are." Of course, "the way things are" is entirely different in other times and places.

Environmentalists and Whole Earth people are making assertions that are still startling to most conventional people. "We're breathing in the air that the Polish people breathed out last week." "We're all passengers, dependent on the life-support system of Spaceship Earth." "Plants, like all living things, respond to love or hate." "*The environment is alive!*" The real estate developer, riding roughshod over the landscape, or the manufacturer dumping his toxic wastes into Lake Superior, doesn't want to hear it.

As we look into any one of the four components of spirit, mind, body, and environment, we find a rich and varied store of data and experience. Together they form a truly magnificent mosaic.

The "personality" is a construct, a mix compounded from these four elements. The amount and flavor which each element contributes varies greatly from person to person. And the mix will also probably vary a good deal over any single person's lifetime.

The word "personality" is derived from the Latin root word *persona*, which was the mask worn by Roman actors that identified which character they were portraying during the performance of a play. This derivation is very apt. People who identify with their personalities will say "my body" and "my mind," and also "my soul". One might well ask them who is this "I" that possesses a body, mind, and soul?

Let us say that John Doe is the personality construct existing at some intersection of our four components. This personality construct has both a subjective reality ("I am John Doe") and an objective reality ("He is John Doe"). In each new lifetime, a new construct is forged out of the four elements. So, in another lifetime, John Doe becomes Mary Jane or Zumakanda. The actor may become temporarily lost in each successive performance. But the consciousness is perennial and always remains to some degree self-aware.

In the spiritual awakening movement there is a fundamental but quite slippery concept: consciousness. I know of no satisfactory definition of the term, yet everyone seems to be aware of being conscious. One could also say we are conscious of being aware, so maybe the two words refer to the same underlying thing. *The American Heritage Dictionary* defines "conscious" as "having an awareness of one's own existence, sensations, and thoughts, and of one's environment," which seems correct as far as it goes. Its Latin root means "participating in knowledge." An interesting and important twist to this is that humans are conscious of being conscious. *They can, therefore, study and manipulate their own consciousness*.

Many related terms arise from such studies and manipulations of consciousness: "unconscious," "subconscious," "consciousness expansion," "superconsciousness," "altered states of consciousness," "collective consciousness," and so on.

The current writings about consciousness (like the writings about love) mostly seem to lack any clearcut definitions. But there are some basic points of agreement in the emerging spiritual picture. One point of strong agreement is that the ordinary human possesses only a thin slice of consciousness, with very little awareness of the levels that exist above and below this slice. Current writers also agree that these other levels, although mostly hidden from awareness, nevertheless influence us continuously and extensively. Thus we are chronically influenced by "unseen forces." This ordinary level of awareness is considered a sort of sleepwalking state.

There is also agreement on a very momentous third point. Through our own efforts we can become *more* conscious of the levels both above and below ordinary awareness, more aware of mind and body, and also more aware of our spiritual nature and the spiritual realms. This is consciousness expansion, and it has been the goal of a thousand and one human disciplines. They have amply demonstrated that it can be done.

In the "lower" direction are the subliminal systems of the mind and the biochemical systems of the body which, taken together, are sometimes referred to as the "lower self" in the mystic literature. For centuries, adepts of various schools have shown remarkable control over these processes, stopping blood flows, going into suspended animation, and performing other such feats. Recent studies have verified that, through biofeedback and physical yoga exercises, individuals can learn to deliberately control such things as blood pressure, heartbeat, brain wave patterns, and temperature in various parts of the body. Reprogramming of lower mind levels through Creative Visualization has successfully alleviated illnesses and refashioned lives. And hypnotic regression has been documented to be successful in bringing to consciousness detailed accurate memories of "forgotten" childhood incidents. So these lower levels *are* accessible, with some work.

Such expansion of awareness "downward" is limited, however, because it merely increases mastery over transitory physical-plane forms. There's nothing wrong with this and it certainly can have its value. But the consciousness expansion that really matters in the long run is "upward": getting in touch with and tuned into our spirituality, our spiritual resonances with others, and with the multidimensional Cosmic All. In this direction are the grandeurs. And wonders. And rescues. And joys. And adventures.

Through "upward" consciousness expansion, an increased awareness of one's mind with its programming, and of one's body with its energy blockages and misalignments, and of the real story of the environment, can occur without too much effort. Each of these components can then be adjusted to create a better life. Negative programmings can be deleted from the mind and old resentments released, to be replaced with more positive affirmations. (*Never* underestimate the transforming power of affirmations.) The energy centers of the body (chakras) can be adjusted and blockages released. And one can take steps to create a more enriched and luxurious environment. At this point, one could well hear a chorus of "Easier said than done." And this is true; there are certainly some barriers and difficulties to be overcome in such an expansion. Expanding one's awareness shares certain qualities with swimming upstream. But it is also easier done than many people realize—after all, millions have done it. *Perhaps the only thing tougher than expanding one's awareness is remaining unaware.* There is also the heartening fact that any small step in the direction of expanded awareness produces innumerable good consequences for the individual and others. I know that all the people around me were very pleased when I lost some of my grimness a few years back.

Expanding your awareness is not just an intellectual exercise. It is a matter of the heart, of feelings and intuitions, much more than a matter of logic. Logic is no more (and no less) than a very useful tool, like a pocket calculator, to help with the process. A person might know all the words and literature of the awakening movement, for instance, and not arrive anywhere without the additional ingredients of heart and soul. For some people (including myself) this has been a difficult, but tremendously rewarding, lesson to learn.

Currently there is quite a bit of physical-plane-oriented research being done on the changes in bodily states that seem to accompany consciousness-expanding experiences. Brain wave alterations and biochemical shifts of various kinds are being studied. These are somewhat fascinating, but they can lead to gross misconceptions. Physical scientists often assert that the body alterations *cause* the consciousness changes, which are only subjective and perhaps hallucinatory. This is backwards reasoning. It is like spotting carrion birds at a battle scene, or perspiration on the face of a lover, and then explaining the battle and the lovemaking by pointing to the buzzards and the sweat. Such assertions leave out just about everything that is meaningful or true about either activity. The body changes and the birds are the incidental *byproducts*, not the causative agents. I personally know of individuals who have been healed from diabetes, crippling back conditions, multiple sclerosis, and cancer, to say nothing of broken hearts and broken lives, through New Age techniques. You might ask *them* if it was "only hallucinatory."

None of the four factors for which this chapter is named can be entirely neglected or denied without producing some imbalance and lopsidedness. A temporary vacation from the environment can be restful, but a permanent withdrawal to a cave, living on nuts and seeds, can make us miss the whole point of being here on the physical plane and only postpone "graduation." An utter emphasis on the body results in a Ken and Barbie doll superficiality, inevitably leading to disappointments and melancholy as the decades pass. Endless preoccupation with the mind is a sort of symbolic autoeroticism, pleasant on occasion, but futile over the long haul. A person who is obsessively concerned with external environmental conditions can become excessively other-directed, having to respond continually to whatever inputs the environment is presently offering. This can really wear one down.

Some people fall into nihilism, rejecting the world as cruel and unjust—no place to bring up children. This karmic position is a virtual guarantee that they will miss what the environment does have to offer. Others feel strongly alienated from their bodies because their body forms don't fit the current fashion in their culture. And some people turn their backs on anything spiritual because of their disavowal of a rigid religious upbringing, or because they once prayed for help and feel their prayers were never answered. The varieties of possible imbalance among the four elements seem endless.

Fortunately, improving any one component can help to eventually uplift and balance the others. Cultivating a healthy body can free the mind from biological problems and increase the likelihood of success in the environment. An enriched and supportive environment can alleviate stresses on the mind, so that the mind will not distort bodily functions. A calm mind can relax the body and aid problem-solving in the environment. Spiritual awakening can provide the energies and loftier viewpoints from which to reprogram the mind into more positive patterns. This can engender more vibrant bodily processes, and, through changed visualizations and behavior, helps produce a more positive environment.

The spirit can directly influence the body through images and energy flows and vibrations. If the channels are open, a spirit in good shape seems to naturally contribute to the health and vibrancy of the body through the high wavelength level of its energy field. It also assists healing, which it seems to know inherently how to do. Less evolved spirits are more clumsy with their bodies. If they are in travail, or receive a severe shock, their disruptive vibrations can depress the immunological system, causing the body to waste away. Remember, all human spirits are still growing and developing. Also, the influence is two-way; the conditions and adventures of the body instantly feed back to the spirit and become part of its permanent repertoire.

When there are open channels among body, mind, and spirit, the spirit can sweep wounds or illnesses away almost with a careless gesture. When there are few connections and many blockages on the flow lines, it seems that any virus or bacteria wandering by can score.

A person's health history is intimately bound up with the quality of interactions among the four components. In the negative direction, this health history is concerned with how sickly and suffering a person is. In the positive direction it is concerned with how physically zestful and expansive the person is. A finding that has been emerging to the point of certainty in recent medical research is that *there is a psychosomatic element to all illnesses*. (It looks like this may also be true for most accidents.) This includes all the grave illnesses which were once thought to be strictly physical. Many conventional doctors are really good-hearted and caring people. But they are intensively trained by the mainstream medical belief structure, with its emphasis on the mechanical technologies of drugs and surgery. So they are often incapable of doing much, if anything, about the negative mental patterns or spiritual travails which lead a person to illness in the first place and prolong its course. Many doctors are now coming to recognize the vital roles played by a patient's mindset and heartset and spirit in the manifesting and outcome of an illness. Unfortunately, however, their techniques remain almost entirely physical-plane manipulations. These mechanical techniques have become pretty good. But, ironically, one of the main effects is that conventional medicine is now able to keep suffering people half-alive almost indefinitely.

Meanwhile, alternative health care approaches are becoming more widely accepted because they are less invasive and less expensive, and they take mental and spiritual factors into account. Anyone who has looked into these alternatives with an open mind knows of the miracle healings they have sometimes produced. I personally know of a number of such cures, some of which were impossible according to conventional medical theory and beliefs. I have personally seen evidence that even a partial spiritual awakening can sometimes produce "magic" in the realms of health. Doctor Bernie Siegel's bestseller, *Love, Medicine, and Miracles*, is filled with wonderful first-hand illustrations of many of these points.

There are, of course, fraudulent healers and psychics. But the New Age certainly has no monopoly on such critters. I have known fraudulent doctors, fraudulent lawyers, fraudulent college professors, fraudulent financial advisors, and fraudulent parents. A minority of fakes and incompetents exists, to the embarrassment of every profession, and does not invalidate the entire profession. Otherwise we would have no valid human endeavors whatsoever.

There are many factors arising from the components of spirit, mind, body, and environment that facilitate illness and sometimes impede its lifting. Deeply woven karmic habit patterns may keep us chronically ill, or on a terminal disease course, unless alleviated. The sickness or accident may be a subliminal ploy for getting love and attention from certain other people. (Sometimes busy parents are only solicitous of their children when they're sick.) We may have planned to undergo such an experience in this lifetime to learn from it. Or we may be utterly unwilling to make the inner mental and spiritual changes that might lead to recovery. We may have *accomplished* whatever we set out to do this time around, and be ready to check out and start another scenario.

Many who finish their life goals or give up on them, and whose friends and family have "gone on," feel ready to end the current incarnation. The loss of life companions and kindred spirits is doubtlessly a major cause of death. Someone clinging desperately to an older parent whose health is failing may, therefore, actually be being selfish and doing a disservice to the parent, who is ready to move on. On the other hand, a strong enough reason to continue living can sometimes be sufficient to revive the clinically dead. A new goal or life purpose seems able to produce miraculous healings of even grave illnesses. The importance of the influence of the will to continue living on the course of human health has now been thoroughly documented. But it raises a deep question. Do you or I have the right to tell people how they should administer their own lives?

Many people find themselves in an uneasy balance between health and illness that persists for years, even decades. One cause of this situation is that they hang suspended between positive and negative beliefs and imagings about themselves. "I'm okay—I'm not doing so well." "We get along—we don't really get along." "My job's all right—I don't really like my job." "I feel pretty good—I don't feel very good." Their health and living experience is consequently also a see-saw. If they just tip the balance a bit in the direction of the positives, the results can be striking. Sometimes a life event, such as falling in love, or pursuing work closer to their life purposes, will do the trick.

Seth points out that it is more the *quality of life* than a matter of sheer survival factors that every consciousness uses in assessing whether to continue living or to discorporate. This is supposedly true for plants and animals as well as people. Some recent social studies lend some empirical support to this contention. It turns out that even people with terminal illnesses can frequently choose their times of death. For instance, they'll wait until after a holiday, or until they've said goodbye to their children.

As for helping others with their health situations, a chorus of New Age professionals have made some startling assertions. One is that, since we all share one another's psychic resonance fields, any spiritual improvement a person experiences also benefits all those around him or her. Higher, healthier wavelengths rub off on others. A second assertion is that you don't beat a disease as you might a competitor; you dissolve and release the imageries and resentments and negativities that produced it in the first place. No exceptions.

A third assertion is that the broadcast of love vibrations can literally dissolve negativity in the body, whether our own or others'. Body trouble spots can be psychically perceived as dark, or dim and flickering, areas. Through such broadcasts, we are all potential healers. The person's own attitudes and intentions are, of course, a main factor here.

There is another avenue through which the spirit and mind can affect general health levels. It is more indirect, but perhaps equally powerful in the long run. A concern and caring about all things great and small seems to grow out of a higher, more positive mental and spiritual vibration level. And this includes caring about the environment. As Barbara Ward points out, we are all passengers on Spaceship Earth, whatever our beliefs or political allegiances. We are all dependent on its life-support systems, just like the crew of the Starship Enterprise. The simple fact is, we've been trashing the planet and we can't do it any more. We're now losing the ozone layer, and researchers have found toxins and pollutants even in the cells of creatures living in Antarctica. So environmental conditions are now looming as a planetary social problem with innumerable health implications, many of which are still unknown. We'll be hearing about these for the rest of our present lifetimes.

Unbeknownst to most people, this process has probably already reached the point where we cannot remain individualistic and self-centered about it. Environmental protection is no longer just a nice idea that businessmen can throw a few dollars toward while they continue to pollute their own children's playgrounds. The negative processes already in motion could provide us all with a near-death experience, which could be a cruel lesson if we insist on learning it the hard way.

As a first cousin to the spiritual awakening movement, there is a diffuse but growing worldwide movement of concern for the environment. Sometimes the same people are involved in both movements, sometimes not. The positive vision it offers is how rich and abundant the environment could be if we used our technologies in an appreciative and supportive manner. Beautiful ambience and abundance for everyone is already within our technical grasp. As always, whatever happens is in our own hands.

At the collective level, there is another environmental issue that may well be the most fundamental and important of them all, affecting health, wealth, lifestyle, and everything else. This issue is the quality of the psychic vibrational field we create for one another. Both hate and love are contagious. Both good news and bad news travel fast and can be infectious. AIDS can spread through the planetary population and so can spiritual awakening. Kindness and unkindness both spread like rumors. Each of us is part of everyone else's environment, physically, mentally, and spiritually. What channels do we tune into? And what channels do we broadcast on?

14

The Journey

From time immemorial, and in a thousand different mystic traditions, the growth of consciousness or spiritual awareness has been described as a *journey*. Since each soul is unique, each person's journey will be unique in many ways. Also each person must choose and map out their own itinerary (again, with a little help from some friends). There are a great many different paths one can take. But whatever path one takes, there are some typical features to the voyage.

Ideally, consciousness expansion is a win-win game, in which my wins are also yours and your wins sweeten my environment, while taking nothing from me except, perhaps, some psychic sludge and negative vibration broadcasts that I can nicely do without. There are some bumps along the road, but a pleasant outcome does seem to be what ultimately happens.

The journey is in some ways similar to climbing the steps of a seawall. As one rises, the view keeps changing and becoming more panoramic. Along the way, all of one's thoughts and realizations should be considered *temporary*, because they're likely to change again after a few more steps. What seems of real value, what is important, and what the traveler feels he or she should do, are also likely to keep changing along the way. So don't just impulsively quit your job or your spouse, or sell your house, without at least sleeping on it. Because tomorrow you might have yet a different view of things. This is not just homespun advice. I have seen people do such things to their later regret, when they subsequently changed their minds again.

A spiritual journey of self-realization is a very real adventure. But, like any adventure, it is not always or entirely comfortable. Some temporary doubts, fears, or even backsliding along the way are almost inevitable. We may have periods when we wonder if we are going crazy. And sometimes others will obligingly tell us that we are. But this, too, is a matter of perspective. *All the evidence suggests that we are far more likely to go crazy if we stay on the treadmill.*

And then there is the important matter of resistance. Over the years, people have expressed to me an astonishing variety of reasons against becoming more spiritually awake. One man was afraid that consciousness-raising would make him a wimp. Another was concerned that he might have to give up R-rated entertainments. A woman was fearful that she wouldn't be as interesting to other people any more. A man was anxious that he might become ineffective in "life's competitive game." Another feared that he might get cancer, because he had read that a famous Christian writer had done so. An older woman said she just wanted to rest in a pine box and find oblivion. One man became angry at the prospect, saying, "I don't want to be a goddamn monk."

Such resistances seem to derive from physical-plane preoccupations, and they show the extent to which the physical plane can have its hooks in people. Perhaps they also demonstrate the reluctance that is often present at the outset of any sort of journey. A journey is always something of an embarking into the unknown. Nor can one forget the force of sheer inertia; after all, journeys always involve change.

Whatever reluctance or fears a person may have, it seems that the spiritual essence possesses an inherent yearning toward growth and development. So, sooner or later, we will choose to set out on a path.

Some sort of inner stirring starts us on the journey into higher consciousness. This stirring is triggered by some occurrence that reminds us, faintly or strongly, that spirituality lies beyond and behind physical things. Sometimes we are not even fully conscious of the stirring at the time, and come to realize its importance only later. Such triggers can be anything—a passage in a book, a beautiful sunrise, the smell of night-blooming jasmine, a dilemma or crisis arising in our lives, or a full-blown near-death visit to the Beyond. Whatever the trigger, it produces a shift, even if ever so slight, in our ordinary focus.

When we set out deliberately on a spiritual journey, we usually encounter a double-bind that at least must be loosened. One set of constraints is personal: the karmic habit patterns and programming examined in previous chapters. We may be set in our ways, riding along on inertia and resistant even to easy changes. For example, try changing something as simple as the time you habitually get up in the morning.

The other set of constraints is composed of our interpersonal network of friends, family, and acquaintances that act as a web of support, but also a web of constraint. For instance, when a child says there's a friendly ghost in the garage, or that he or she (who has never been there in this lifetime) remembers England and how the horses smelled in the barn, a chorus of grownups will tell the child that he or she has an overactive imagination and there are no such things. Especially in the Western world, we do a pretty good job of keeping one another focused on the physical plane as the "real world." In this negative sense, we are to some extent each other's keepers.

The two parts of this double-bind often reinforce each other. They operate to "keep us in our place" to some degree. But still, there was that spiritual stirring . . . .

When we take a few spiritual steps, a flareup in our interpersonal network often arises. A change in our perspectives and wavelengths, even if nothing is said, can upset the established stability of the network, and create some reverberations and backlashes. In most cases, the other people involved aren't deliberately or maliciously trying to hold us back. It's just that karmic patterns of individuals strongly tend to interface with each other, so that a shift in awareness can shake up the patterns of all concerned.

Conventional people claim a degree of "ownership" of one another. This is blatantly expressed in many popular songs, such as "You Belong

To Me," "My Girl," "You're Mine," and so on. We speak of my spouse, my child, my mother, *my* friend, using the posessive form of speech and meaning it. So changes in a person's habit patterns, perspectives, and vibration levels are sometimes perceived by the "owners," consciously or unconsciously, as threatening. There may be fear of losing the relationship, fear the relationship will change in unknown ways, or jealousy that the person is showing independence and turning elsewhere.

As Barbara Clow has noted, since we are often involved with people we have known before in previous lives, our own changes challenge them to look at other levels of their own selves. For example, if a wife goes onto the spiritual path, her husband may uneasily remember losing her to it before.

Sometimes the "owner" will be very supportive of the person's journey, or even actively join in. This can produce a renewed and enhanced companionship and shared interest, and a mutual growth. Sometimes the relationship will not withstand the strain of the changes and will dissolve. This outcome usually happens when the journeyer is too hasty in changing everything, or when the relationship was based on low vibration levels in the first place. For instance, a person who moves out of a partying lifestyle will often be dropped by most of his or her former companions. I have seen this occur several dozen times.

Such potential flareups present the person with a problem: should they push forward and handle the flak, or settle back and not rock any boats? The fledgling journeyer may feel that, either way, he or she is going to lose to some extent. This dilemma is a major reason why people often vacillate back and forth between the old ways and the new during the early stages of their journeys. The grip of one's interpersonal networks can be strong, involving economic, social, and emotional considerations. After all, it was no accident that the person had formed those particular interpersonal ties. No doubt a Like Attracts Like factor was at work. But now the person is changing.

Technically speaking, the journey seems to be in good part a matter of changing the vibrational levels or wavelengths in which one operates, or at least expanding the width of the spectrum one operates on. Such changes will virtually guarantee many new experiences for the person undergoing them. Some of the person's associates may feel they have "lost" the person when such changes happen, and in a sense they have. At least they have lost the physical-plane manifestation of the person they were habituated to. No one would deny the real difference between interacting with a self-centered competitive person and an open-hearted loving one. But the jousting, competitive manifestation might have been the real basis for the relationship.

In all fairness, we should try to understand the situation of those associated with the journeyer. They often like some of the changes the person is manifesting—less irritable, more considerate and understanding, for instance—but they are changes. The changed vibration levels may be literally beyond them, so they can't understand what's going on. The changes are noticeable and real. A guy isn't as aggressive and macho; a woman isn't as interested in getting stoned and partying; a man becomes less concerned about making money. Boyfriends, girlfriends, companions, and family can become puzzled and uneasy. Some of the people around the new voyager may jump aboard and go along on the journey, but never all of them. Some mutual estrangements are almost inevitable.

As these shifts are occurring, another interpersonal aspect of the journey is probably unfolding. When we begin operating on different wavelengths and with new perspectives, there are likely to be encounters with new people who are operating on compatible levels. This usually leads to some shifts in the makeup of our network, with some former companions dropping out and some new ones being added. In extreme cases, a whole new interpersonal network along with a new career and new close ties may result. For instance, there is some suggestion that the incidence of divorce and new romantic arrangements is higher than ordinary among near-death-experience veterans. Similar interpersonal shifts are, of course, also likely if one slides downward into operating at coarser vibrational levels, as in turning to a lifestyle of debauchery.

So as we progress along on a spiritual journey, we don't "fit in" in the same way as before, and we are likely to break with established interpersonal patterns. We can, however, establish new patterns with the same people, and often this amounts to an upgrade with fewer false fronts and more genuine compassion. This can be a relief and release for everyone concerned. I know of people who *finally* established a loving and honest relationship with their parents only after years of consciousness-expansion work. Any ties that are truely based on spiritual connectedness are evidently never lost in the long run.

So any interpersonal problems of the new journeyer are softened and potentially transformed by the gains made along the way. There is more light and aliveness in one's life, and from this, many good things can follow.

A journey into spiritual awakening is seldom, if ever, a smooth, straight-line progression. This is true even if the person is able to pursue it wholeheartedly and singlemindedly—which is seldom the case. There are usually periods of "nothing happening," moments of doubt and depression, earth-plane distractions and temptations to give it up, along with moments of grandeur and illumination that can be almost too uplifting to bear. But these kinds of ups and downs are usually part of *any* human endeavor, such as starting a business, or raising a family. *The thing about spiritual awakening is that the rewards are less transitory than in any other human endeavor.* And you *do* get to take them with you.

The journey is usually marked by surprises. A technique that was miraculous for others doesn't seem to work for you; there are sudden moments of feeling great; old psychological wounds surface; periods occur when nothing seems to be happening (but it is). There are incubation periods while new conceptions "sink in"; periods of confusion as old belief structures break apart and new ones are forming; moments when nothing seems to make sense and moments when you seem to understand everything. You notice a light fixture on the ceiling or a bush at the corner of the house, as if for the first time. You catch a real glimpse of the inner life of another person. There are questions; psychic tinglings and itches; reclusive withdrawals from external noises so you can hear yourself. You feel a bit like a puppy breaking out of the yard. You have strange, half-remembered dreams. I vividly remember losing my fear of death, and then discovering that I was afraid of living.

A spiritual journey is a progressive unfolding, so it takes some time. Impatience is certainly understandable, but it tends to set up disharmonies and tensions that can impede the process. But compared to many other human endeavors, it really doesn't take so long to begin to make progress. For instance, it takes four years to get a Bachelor of Arts diploma, let alone an advanced degree. And we're considering major spiritual shifts that cannot occur in a day. But they needn't take decades or lifetimes, either. Beings on both sides of the veil agree that there can be a tremendous amount of spiritual development within one lifetime; enough to lift us up and away from the road we were plodding along, and to open up breathtaking new vistas and options.

Each individual's path is unique in some way and can differ markedly from others. So exploring to find our own way is one of the things that takes some time. We might spend years in a convent or a cult, for instance, before transcending its limitations and applying the lessons learned elsewhere. Teachers and guides, advice and invitations, all can help. But, ultimately, we must both design and experience our own road.

The progressive unfolding has some other interesting aspects. Our process with a new idea or concept such as rebirth, or that our beliefs create our realities, will typically go through something like the following cycle:

One: Resistance; the idea is weird, far out, unbelievable, too much, *wrong.*

Two: The idea is thought provoking; maybe explains some things, but is a bit far-fetched. Maybe. (S-t-r-e-t-c-h)

Three: The idea brings realizations, illuminations, and new alignments of thought; so that's what's going on. *Aha!*

Four: We accept the notion and it becomes part of our repertoire; *well, of course.*

Then the growth continues. A new idea comes along, such as "all plants and animals have their own form of consciousness," or "no lifetime is ever wasted," and we go through the cycle again.

As we grow in consciousness, words can change and grow in the meanings they hold for us. We discover that common words contain buried beliefs which have been slanting and limiting our perspectives. For instance, our mainstream "God" is very male, sits on a throne with harps playing around him (not electric guitars), and is an irritable and dominating parent who demands obedient children and will not be crossed.

Then there are the prevailing conceptions of "love." A thousand popular songs talk about a love that boils down to sexual ownership and access and dependence, in *very* conditional forms. Their real titles might be "I Really Want to Screw You and Own You," and "Go Ahead and Ravish Me So I Can Lay Claim to You." It is no accident that the word "possess" has both a sexual and ownership meaning in common usage.

Our personal conception of such words deepens and transmutes, and may continue to change again and again as we proceed. Books we once read or ideas we've heard can grow and take on different meanings, too. And we experience the same old physical-plane phenomena, such as trees, or the wind, or a warm room, in a different, more multidimensional way. *If you want to change the world you experience, just change your consciousness level.* In this way you can discover a new environment all around you.

Many of the truths about things spiritual are so easy to say, like the Golden Rule—"Do unto others as you would have them do unto you"—which is indeed golden. But they can be so difficult to really grasp and apply. Because of our strong physical-plane focus and sleepy awareness, we must sometimes reach a certain level of consciousness before we really "hear" such truths. But perhaps such messages never fall on entirely deaf ears.

There is another experience awaiting the new traveller that tends to produce both temporary despair and permanent enlightenment. As we begin to gain some expanded awareness, and take a look from this new vantage point at our past and present behavior and games, we may not like the picture very much. From an even slightly higher perspective, we can often begin to see the pettiness, the selfishness, the deceit, and even the vindictiveness of some of our daily actions and thoughts. We can also catch glimpses of some of the consequences of these thoughts and actions for ourselves and others. This process seems to be something of an earthly equivalent of the "life review" reported as a common element in near-death experiences and between-lives sojourns. Expanded perceptions include greater perceptiveness of ourselves.

With this new, expanded view of our doings, we may well go through a temporary period of self recrimination, feeling like a worm, if not a son of a bitch. Sometimes we will take one such look and decide to sink back down for awhile into being a spiritual couch potato. However, there seems to be something of a spiritual safety valve operating here: we will take on only as much enlightenment as we can handle at any one time. If we just hang on and go through the process of adjustment to new perspectives, the results can be cathartic and exhilarating, if a little humbling. Somewhere along the line, we begin to learn to quit being so judgmental and to just forgive and care for ourselves and for others. It's not necessary to cast any stones, even at oneself.

Because of all these inner and interpersonal factors, a journey of spiritual awakening takes awhile. It takes awhile for all the realizations and gains to sink in through the layers of our total beings. It takes awhile to release and dissolve some of the deeply ingrained habits and resentments and programming, and to transcend some of our dearly held illusions. It takes awhile to go through the experiences and gather together the lessons of Earth School. We must progress to a certain point before we are ready, or even able, to perceive and handle further growth opportunities. But the journey is not really long in the scheme of things, when measured against eternity. And then there is the intriguing notion that there is actually a great progression of journeys, in which this journey is partly a preparation for the next journey . . . and the next . . . .

From the foregoing pages, a journey of consciousness growth and spiritual awakening might seem like a lot of work and hassle. Someone might possibly ask, "Why do it?" This question could be answered in many different ways, such as, "You're on the journey anyway, so you might as well take some conscious control of the process." Or, "Consider the alternatives!" Or, "How many millennia do you want to spend drinking beer and watching baseball?" Or, "How many times do you want to get born and married and buried?"

The most down-to-earth answer to this "Why bother?" question might be to summarize some of the gains reported by those who have achieved some awakening, and observed by those around them:

They feel more alive and zestful, and feel they are inhabiting a living environment that is rich in experiences and sensations. Boredom and weariness are no longer their constant companions. Others say they are much more lively than before.

They are happier more of the time, and are having more fun than they used to have. Others say they are more interesting and fun to be around.

They are more flexible, more able to adapt to changing local circumstances and roll with the times. Others say that things don't get them down so much now.

They feel more tuned in, harmonious, and connected with the people around them, and they enjoy other people more now. Others feel they are more understanding and supportive, and less egocentric than most other people.

They are more lighthearted and high-spirited. They laugh more easily and about more things, including themselves and their own manifestations. Others say they take themselves less seriously and are less touchy.

They are not immune to illness, but they are less prone to it. They often don't catch the flu when it's going around. When hurt or sick, they tend to recover quickly, sometimes "miraculously". Health professionals remark on their vitality.

They are not immune to setbacks or disasters, but they do seem to lead a bit of a charmed life. When such things do befall them, they seem to take them more in stride and survive them better. Others are sometimes surprised at how untroubled they seem.

They display frequent flashes of psychic sensitivity of one sort or another. Others say they often have a sixth sense about things.

They are more conscious of, and therefore harmonious with, the rhythms and flows of their surroundings. Others say they seem to be able to fit in easily almost anywhere if they want to.

They are more competent. They deliver their share on jobs and agreements, without accidentally dumping all the computer data or leaving messes of one kind or another for others to handle. Others say they are easier to work with.

They are more appreciative. A small gesture, a cool breeze, an interesting comment, is less likely to be lost on them. Others are often surprised at how much they habitually notice and enjoy even "little things."

They find life meaningful. They broadcast a sense of being involved in something important, and of going somewhere. Others remark that they are sometimes envious of this.

Certainly none of these are hard and fast characteristics, nor are all of them manifested all the time. They are just very strong tendencies which many investigators, including myself, have noticed. These and similar attributes are also a matter of degree, since spiritual awakening is itself a matter of degree, and doesn't operate like an on-off switch. Nor are people on spiritual paths necessarily saintly—to me they seem to have more in common with the high elves.

A spiritual journey, like any venture, is partly a balance of costs and rewards. What will it take and what are the returns? But, in this case, the ordinary rules of left-brain logic and bookkeeping are soon left far behind. How much are a lighter heart, a clearer head, and an awakened deathless spirituality worth?

The flowering of any consciousness is a celebration. This fact leads us into a couple of very important points about journeys that are often hard to grasp and hold onto in the face of physical-plane inputs and standards. The first is that spiritual evaluations can differ markedly from society's. Those steeped in a physical-plane focus might find it hard to understand why a wise being who has reached the old soul level might choose to be a forester or civil servant, rather than seek the international acclaim he or she might easily achieve. The tremendous growth and influence of such a person might go entirely unrecognized by young souls hotly pursuing physical-plane success.

Another point is that we cannot judge others' paths on the basis of our own. An intellectual learned in the literature about things spiritual, or a New Age celebrity, is not necessarily in any way "ahead" of a simple girl working in a pet hospital who broadcasts loving warmth to the animals and their "owners"; or a single parent raising four children against circumstantial odds and dramatically assisting in the flowering of their potentials. One of the hardest lessons to learn seems to be that other people don't have to see *your* light in order to evolve. Nor is enlightenment a competitive, "more evolved than thou" game.

Those involved in the worldwide awakening are in different stages of development and expansion. There are veterans and there are newcomers, still learning some of the basic ideas and jargon, and asking the questions the veterans once asked. And those who have transcended the physical plane are also evolving in different stages, continuing along in *their* journeys. So, in an ultimate sense, it seems we are *all* fellow travellers.

15

Some Spiritual Pitfalls

Every kind of journey is fraught with potential problems and pitfalls, and a voyage into spiritual awakening is no exception. The neophyte can have exaggerated fears about such pitfalls, like the medieval sailors who feared they would be devoured by sea monsters or that they would fall off the edge of the world. The new voyager may also know little or nothing about the *real* pitfalls which do exist and so stumble into them unawares while busily warding off nonexistent beasties. Therefore it seems worthwhile to look at some of the actual problems one can run into on the spiritual journey and some remedies for them.

Any exploration of the spiritual is, in the last analysis, a *personal* trip. Only the individual can sort through the available channels and false trails to find his or her own pathway. Happily, this can be done without undue apprehension, because even if mistakes are made they may provide a valuable learning experience. For instance, many exmembers of fringe cults that I have talked to have told me they learned a lot from the cult experience and are much the wiser for it now. It seems that any spiritual venture produces growth gains.

People beginning on the road to spiritual expansion, where there are few signposts or roadmaps, can, like innocents or amateurs in any field, be somewhat at the mercy of those claiming to be more advanced and more professional. Even when these are good-hearted and well-meaning beings (and the majority are), there is still the danger that the novice, who is in a poor position to judge, may have a spiritual dogma imposed upon him or her. This isn't necessarily bad, because it can provide the person with some stability and direction while getting his or her act together, just as training wheels can help a child learn to ride a bike. Problems can arise if the religion, discipline, or cult attempts to "capture" the new explorer, and to program him or her to accept *only* their version of the cosmos, complete with dire warnings about what happens to those who stray from *their* path. This is a complex matter, because the dogma may indeed embody many spiritual truths along with the dross. There are two main remedies suggested by many teachers in this area. First, only follow a person, discipline, or book when it feels right for you, and be prepared to change when it no longer feels right. And second, as Wayne Hatford, Shakti Gawain, and other New Age writers suggest, follow your heart, gut feelings, and head, in that order, and you're likely to come out all right.

These two points will help the explorer steer an appropriate personal course. In addition there are three main danger signs that should give anyone pause. If a person or group wants large sums of money, if a person or organization indulges in heavy name calling toward alternative paths, and if there is heavy aggrandizement of a human leader, you can suspect that something other than spiritual enlightenment is going on. Note that the great spiritual leaders throughout the ages asked for only modest material support, were superhumanly tolerant of others, and displayed an awesome degree of humility. The many genuine avenues for spiritual development do not require that you refinance your house, or bow in self-deprecation to a fellow human being. And any place can serve as a spiritual temple, including your bathtub, or a tree in your back yard. *You and the light can reach one another anywhere in the cosmos*.

There is another pitfall that is more strictly psychological. By definition, paranormal experiences are not ordinary, at least from a physical-plane viewpoint. In the words of the psychologist William James, they are ineffable, that is, indescribable and untranslatable into ordinary language. Those actively seeking consciousness expansion are venturing into the unknown, and there seems to be an almost universal human tendency to be both excited and fearful when confronted with the new and strange, whether it's a first date or an encounter with the spiritual. How one *responds* to the experience is very much determined by one's prior mindset. If we've been conditioned to fear the unknown, then any surprise, psychic or mundane, can be upsetting, even when we are reaching for it.

Unfortunately, we have been programmed with many dark notions about the spiritual, even if we don't consciously embrace them. "It was a dark and stormy night . . . " has been the opening image for countless tales of supernatural terror that are told around campfires, in books and movies, and on television. The paranormal has a shivery reputation and has remained a fashionable (and profitable) way of frightening people for centuries. This adds up to a lot of negative programming and a lot of negative vibrations. Storytellers give us dark and scary tales; but veterans of actual paranormal experience give us almost entirely uplifting reports of universal light and love and wisdom.

Zealous churchmen have sometimes added to this negativity by maligning "the supernatural and the occult" as demonic realms which should be left alone by the wise and the decent. Aside from anything else, such pronouncements entirely ignore the fact that the spiritual realm is our *home territory*. (It is also noteworthy that the Bible is alleged to be a "channeled" book.)

Residues of such conditioning can combine with a person's own doubts and fears to add an unnecessary darker coloration to the reality of a spiritual experience, even among those seeking the light. How this works can be seen from an example that has happened to many. Through some consciousness-raising technique, a person has become more sensitive spiritually, and senses a presence by their bedside at night. From our accumulated evidence, the highest probability is that this is a discarnate family member or friend. It might also just be a restless spirit wandering around. Chances are very, very slight that it is really malevolent or mischievous. *But, so what, even if it is?* You can simply tell it to go, or visualize your favorite sacred symbols and flow them toward it, or call upon a friendly, more evolved spirit to remove and possibly help it. But, whatever the objective facts, the person with lingering fears of the supernatural may react with fright and shock even toward the spirit of a loved one. Many earthbound spirits that people find scary are not at all evil—they are just distressed or upset about something. If you want to take your courage in hand, you can get into communication with them and often talk them through their difficulty. Who knows, you may make a friend in the process, and it never hurts to have friends. (Remember, everyone has friends on the astral planes.)

In terms of innocence and the unknown, there are a couple of hazardous side journeys people should be warned about. The milder of these is attempting to develop ESP—or psychic abilities—without also increasing one's spiritual level. This is a haphazard and superficial endeavor at best, since such abilities ultimately flow from one's spiritual essence. To attempt to develop and use such abilities in a manipulative way, where one person's winning is someone else's loss, is an abuse which seems to have a built-in boomerang effect in the long run.

One acquaintance of mine became interested in out-of-body techniques, with the hope of having intrusive astral sex with girls who had turned a cold shoulder toward him in physical life. Another man looked into ESP and crystals as possible means of becoming more successful at selling a semi-fraudulent product. In both cases there was no concern about the consent or well being of the potential recipients. Neither individual was successful.

Advertisements in psychic brochures and magazines, or dime-store mystic books, often pander to such intentions. The come-on is that you will be able to satisfy your lusts and have power over others if you send them your money. "Trap Him with Your Psychic Powers." "I'll Cast Any Spell for You." "Use ESP to Win the Lottery." "Our Pulsing Gemstones Will Bring You Love". Lonely and stranded people are drawn to such advertisements and they deserve compassion. But mysticism without heart and soul is about as empty as you can get. The magic is in conscious expansion of one's spiritual essence.

A second kind of side journey can be a more serious matter. Pursuit of the dark side of the Force or the "left hand path" is almost inevitably a game that everyone loses. It is not fatal for the spiritual essence; nothing is. And one may learn lessons (such as *don't do it*). But it can lead to temporary retrogression and greatly prolong the evolutionary climb. There are no actual demons as such, but trafficking with less evolved beings and the low levels of the astral planes engenders little joy or light or love. And since such actions can inhibit the growth of others, the end result is to needlessly increase one's karmic burdens. To put it mildly, the lower astral levels are not as pleasant as the higher ones.

Whether we walk the dark side or the light side, we influence the reality of other people. The manner in which you influence others rebounds in turn upon you, because they make up part of your psychic field. If such influences are positive, this is wonderful. If negative, however, you suffer some of the "flash-burn" consequences you are helping to create. This is one reason why hatred and resentment are so insidious and self-defeating.

The world is full of leaders, experts, guides, and gurus offering to help others with the spiritual side of things. They claim special knowledge, skills, and powers in these realms. From the dawn of history, people have been flocking to them for assistance, enlightenment, and perhaps escape from their circumstances. Many of these leaders and authorities have been sincere; others have not. Some have really been able to assist and succor humanity; many have not. When we step back and take a detached look, it seems that only a minority have been able to help others without any hooks, lines, or sinkers.

It would be foolish to uncritically recommend all workers in the paranormal field, because disciplines vary in effectiveness, and practitioners within any particular discipline vary in competence and degree of spiritual advancement. Also, there is the personal factor of what is right for a specific person at a specific stage of his or her journey. But beyond this there are certain potential pitfalls for both unwary leaders and their followers. Anyone familiar with these areas has seen some of these pitfalls in action. The factor that underlies these pitfalls seems to be the very low level of spiritual awareness of most incarnate human beings at this time. All of us are innocents abroad. The typical human being, based in a body and enmeshed in the physical plane, frequently feels lost, timid, even terrified, like a young animal on its own in the wilds or a child lost in a shopping mall. Such humans are *vulnerable*. And, being vulnerable, they are sometimes gullible.

In such a state of vulnerability, people who are drawn to the spiritual aspects of reality don't know where to turn. In such a condition, they will frequently just buy into one of the pre-packaged dogma systems at hand in their culture, since it seems to contain answers and some echoes of universal truth. They may also come under the influence of a charismatic human who comes along and offers them some anchorage and security, and a Way.

Many people come under the spell of someone who professes to be above the ordinary in spiritual awareness and ability, be they cult leader, tribal shaman, or minister of a prevailing religion. It seems that there are so few clear signposts in these realms that people flock to anyone who has a bit more knowledge (or arrogance) than themselves.

For the lure of a bit of spiritual awareness, a few direct experiences, and the promise of more, people will pay out vast sums of money and devote years of their lives to various cults and sects. This is a testimony to how spiritually hungry people really are. It is easy to sit back and take pot shots at such groups and their members, who can, indeed, get temporarily captured within the bubble of a cult's social and psychological world. But the companionship and the intensity of the cause, and the sense of belonging, can give members a sense of aliveness and purpose not so easily come by on the streets or in the suburbs of mainstream society. Can one find wisdom in such groups? Of course. Can one find wisdom without them? Of course.

Certainly a human spiritual leader and his or her group can provide some guidance and inspiration for the newcomer. New vistas may open up and a new language for communicating about the supernatural will be there. There will be fellow companions on the voyage. New members may feel that they have found a haven, and a group of kindred spirits, and a cause and a faith. And perhaps they have in truth found all these things. This can be the case whether the group is composed of a handful of locals or is a worldwide religion.

In examining pitfalls, we must sharply distinguish between the manifesting of a spiritual force, the preserved scriptures and dogma pertaining to this manifestation, and the human leaders and ministers representing the force and scriptures. These are three different things. For instance, we know from historical documentation that the scriptures of most major religions have been repeatedly edited and tampered with by subsequent human generations. And humans have undertaken a thousand and one wretched enterprises in the name of the Prince of Peace.

The leader has almost always had some direct psychic experiences, usually of a profound, life-changing nature. During the experience, the leader-to-be, for example, may have had the overwhelming sensation that the universe was filled with an intense, spiritual blue light. In interpolating these experiences into human terms, the leader develops a dogma—some explanation of the occurrence and some techniques for spiritual improvement. He or she is likely to feel that they have found *the* answer rather than *an* answer, and have seen *the* light rather than *a* light. At this point, the fledgling leader may feel messianic about telling others of his or her enlightenment. He or she may have seemingly boundless energy, enthusiasm, and certainty, and with these attributes can sweep aside the snickers and yawns of others with a tolerant wave of the hand. Their high-spirited preaching is often infectious, and others begin to be drawn into the vision. And so the Church of the Blue Light is born.

If the fledgling leader persists, those who continue to listen become a circle or flock, with the leader as the superordinate. The leader may claim that the dogma is a fundamentally new revelation or a new and necessary reform of prevailing practices. The following may remain small and strictly local, or may grow to international proportions. The dogma may seem weird and laughable to non-members, but to the followers it becomes *gospel*.

The group comes to develop what sociologist Everet Hughes called "a little world of their own," with distinctive rituals, customs, argot, and worldviews. The leader is, far and above, the major force in designing this little world, and, to be a real member, a follower must at least partially inhabit it.

Meanwhile, the follower is often undergoing a transforming personal experience, perhaps discovering new meaning in a formerly aimless existence. Psychosomatic ills may fall away by the carload. Listlessness is replaced by bright eyed fervor; the person feels *alive*.

Virtually any spiritual discipline can produce strong personal experiences for some individuals because they all touch upon common higher principles. Even one of these experiences, if intense enough, will tend to bond the person to the group, the dogma, and its leaders. The fact that many other disciplines could have produced similar results is not known to the enthralled follower. A spiritual awakening is an awesome experience for an individual, however it is brought about. This is not to say that all disciplines are equal in effectiveness, just that all can sometimes produce profound results.

Having had direct personal experience with the supernatural, the vast majority of leaders are sincere. The leader must have a goodly amount of inner strength to survive and to steer his or her group along. But the very fact that the leader marches to a different drummer, in Thoreau's words, is simultaneously his or her strength and a potential pitfall for all concerned.

Who is there in this typical group setup to run "quality control" on the leader? Whatever he or she says goes, except for those members who dissent enough to leave or be thrown out. No follower is an equal. Leaders of other groups, even within the same mystic tradition, do not share in this group's little world, so they are not considered peers in most respects. In most instances, the leader must be his or her own editor, counselor, and critic—a formidable task for any human being. The leader may have a few lieutenants as confidants to talk to, but these are still his or her juniors, and the history of movements shows how precarious these positions are in the long run. The leader may have direct spirit guidance, but these higher transmissions are subject to the leader's all-too-human filterings, interpretations, and distortions.

In this state of exalted aloneness, it is easy for the leader to fall prey to self-aggrandizement and delusion. Both the leader and his or her followers come to regard the leader's comments as pronouncements, and the leader's possibly valid insights as doctrines. A process of elevation both by the self and followers may set in. The supernatural is a tricky realm, as we've seen, not easily captured with human concepts. The leader, bereft of any peer review, and by now perhaps his or her own most enchanted listener, can lose the way without even realizing it.

Followers are expected to look up to the leader, and they may come to worship him or her to some extent, as a being much more wise and spiritually elevated than themselves. This tendency further increases the members' dependency and spiritual other-directedness. The leader, in turn, can become intoxicated with this adulation. At this point, the leader has been given a good deal of interpersonal power. If he or she comes to view the followers as personal minions in the cause, while becoming further ego-inflated by their worship, the leader may unintentionally fall prey to his or her own rhetoric. The leader may come to feel justified in simply *using* the followers. And since they hold him or her in such high esteem and adoration, a good many may delight in being used. This using may take virtually any form and tends to have no bounds. The handing over of all one's worldly possessions is not uncommon; the doing of heinous deeds in the name of a great cause, and personal or sexual servicing are not unknown. Meanwhile the group's techniques may continue to produce at least intermittent spiritual experiences.

As all of these developments are unfolding, the group is likely to be beset by an additional pitfall. Inevitably, the leader and members will be subjected to some criticism and rejection from the surrounding society, and they may experience discrimination and outright repression. The human tendency is to hit back at the "persecutors," and to adopt a separatist dogma dividing the world into the believers versus everyone else. There are also the frustrations of trying to win over nonmembers to the group. There tends to be further distancing from those who won't come along. And so, a group experiencing intolerance and rejection comes to be intolerant and rejecting of others. The writings of one of the newer religious sects, for instance, are shot through with pronouncements condemning government officials, members of other movements, newsmen, social scientists, nonmembers, anyone who questions the leader's doctrines, and even its own followers who are not wholehearted and zealous enough.

We now have all the ingredients for several scenarios. When two such groups, steeped in their own righteousness, meet and clash, we can have a Holy War, as has happened hundreds of times in history and is currently happening in several parts of the world. The Church of the Blue Light and the Church of the Green Leaf devastate one another. (How did they miss the fact that blue lights and green leaves together make a beautiful morning?)

Even when holy wars are avoided, there is another common scenario in which the group closes ranks against nonmembers and descends into entrenched negativity toward other spiritual disciplines and the society at large. Strong sectarian right-wrong, we-them attitudes become part of the group's dogma and members must learn these "proper" attitudes, which involve a fundamental violation of the connectedness of all beings. Any spiritual group which sets itself apart from others is virtually guaranteeing its own eventual decline into sectarianism and cant. The usual outcome is that the group becomes fossilized, and then factions within it break away in search of more direct spiritual experience. This historical process has already produced large numbers of competing sects within all of the world's major established religions.

Occasionally a whole group can go off the rails and develop a sort of collective madness. Since group members associate more and more with one another and less and less with outsiders, errant tendencies of the leader can get reinforced and magnified. This can happen to the point where the whole group engages in extreme practices such as the mass suicide of Jonestown, or the self-mutilations of some medieval cults. When there are few if any checks from within or from outside, on the road the group takes, this road may end up anywhere.

A happier scenario is one where the group evolves, growing collectively wiser and more skillful in addressing spiritual things. This evidently happened among Tibetan Buddhist and Franciscan monks, and the Kabbalists, for example. And it seems to be happening in the New Age movement, as we will see. Tolerance of other views and a recognition of spiritual universality seem to be two major ingredients fostering this more benign outcome. A third factor seems to be the avoidance of physical-plane politics.

There are also gurus who deliberately strive to guide, then graduate and free their followers. Some spiritually evolved people also do not form groups, and, from personal inclination or spiritual belief, refuse to have subordinates. They may guide an informal circle of other seekers, but resist any further elevation. One such person I spoke with said he was an old soul who was both weary and wary of the hassles and traps of the physical plane. He said he'd had enough, and I believe he meant it, in every meaning of the phrase. He certainly never did any advertising.

The individual members of a spiritual group will differ in the degree to which they are attracted to either the compassionate, universal side of the group's dogma or its more doctrinaire, sectarian aspects. *Both* traditions exist within each of the major world religions and they are sometimes in open conflict, as in the medieval Catholic church and present-day Islam. The first focus seems most in tune with our emerging New Age picture: compassion versus catechism, acceptance versus zeal, and so on. According to which is emphasized, the same religious denomination can therefore include both many Mother Teresas and also many torturing inquisitors.

It might be easy to condemn many group leaders and their spellbound followers. But we should also leave some room for compassion. A brave spirit originally set out on a voyage of discovery and some other people took the risk and jumped aboard, for better or worse. These followers found some sort of haven, at least for awhile, which is nothing to sneer at on the physical plane. No doubt some spiritual stirrings occurred. And no doubt everyone concerned learned some lessons, which, the high level spirits tell us, are never lost. So, in the final, reckoning, everybody may have won.

16

What To Do?

There are a lot of thought provoking and even enthralling notions surrounding the idea of spiritual awakening. But what does one *do*? How does one go about moving from idle curiosity into actively doing something about personal development?

A few people have created a life situation where they have the time, the resources, and the freedom from physical-plane ties to single-mindedly and wholeheartedly pursue their spiritual growth. This is not so for the vast bulk of the world's current population, who are pretty well immersed in just surviving and keeping their lives together. Even in advanced technological societies with a relatively high standard of living, most people feel up against it, in one way or another, most of the time. So they may defer any serious spiritual questing until they finish their degree, or raise their children, or get established in a career, or whatever.

The fact that it doesn't have to be this way, individually or collectively, is an insight not easily available to them in the midst of their daily strivings and preoccupations. Powerful spiritual truths, shouted down to them from those at higher awareness levels, can too easily get lost in the noise of physical living and the echoes of distance. And they shout back (often correctly), "But you don't see the crosses I have to bear." It is true that more enlightened beings, who have made it at least partly out into the light, can sometimes lose sight of the jarring intensity of living in coarser, dimmer vibration levels. What may now be so easy for the more evolved to understand and do, may be hard for less evolved beings, entangled in lower wavelengths, to even hear.

Most people, at this point, do not feel they have the wherewithal to pursue any consciousness-expansion program that is either very elaborate or very expensive. This can create something of a vicious circle: they cannot look up from their lives to higher vistas which might help free them from being so locked into these very same lives. Fortunately, this situation is far from hopeless, *because there are things anyone can do.* And spirituality is so powerful that doing anything at all results in progress and brings about changes in one's life.

In spiritual endeavors, people often look for dramatic and profound happenings. But even a *slight* nudge will result in changing the course of a person's life, just as a slight nudge of the controls of an airplane will lead to altering its flight trajectory and destination. The more slight nudges, the faster and more extensive the course alterations. For instance, if you did nothing else than get a family to say a cheerful "good morning" to one another every day, this would significantly uplift their family life over time. Or if you could get someone to just pause a few moments instead of automatically lashing back at sarcastic and disagreeable remarks, this would sweeten that person's environment. Or if someone learned to delete a couple handfuls of negative thoughts every day, they might well experience improved health within a few weeks. None of these things costs anything or takes Herculean effort. But such "nudges" make a difference.

As one begins, there seems to be a difficult first step in any self-development program. How do we get up enough self-discipline to start on some regimen to increase our self-discipline? How do we get our minds under enough control to pursue a course in mind control? How do we overcome negative, "it won't work" attitudes in order to implement a plan to curb negativities?

Such seemingly Catch-22 problems may, understandably, make us despair. But, again, the answer is that *doing anything* will result in some progress. So have heart. Just being *aware* of some phenomena, like the power of negative thinking, begins to undermine its force. For instance, you may read a charming and uplifting book about positive emotions or the power of unconditional love and then lash out at someone the next morning, causing more negativity in your environment. But this time you are *aware* that you did so because of deep-rooted patterns. This is growth. One of these days you won't lash out. As you become aware of such patterns, they begin to lose their commanding force. We can grow through noticing how we *feel*. When you get angry or upset, notice what the context is and who you are around. Wisdom dissolves karma.

The available spiritual books, workshops, tapes, and courses contain literally thousands of consciousness-raising techniques and exercises, but they are not all the same, not all equal. They vary greatly in the ease or difficulty of doing, and in their simplicity or complexity. They also vary in how steeped in dogma they are. For instance, you can meditate or do positive affirmations as part of some particular denominational religious ritual, or you can just meditate and do positive affirmations. Underneath it all, any positive thought or intention, such as "I do well," or "It's a nice day," is an affirmation.

The available techniques also vary in how well they resonate with each person in his or her current stage of evolution. This is why writers and teachers of the awakening movement advise: If a technique feels right for you, do it; if it doesn't feel right, don't do it.

Looking around at the position of most people in our present society, I can suggest a few simple and basic things that virtually anyone can do, even though they have little money or time to spare. Although these actions are utterly simple, they are extremely powerful and have already transformed millions of lives. These seem to be some of the "bottom-lines" of spiritual awakening. There are, of course, no ironclad guarantees for these suggestions, and I must make the obligatory defensive disclaimer that they in no way constitute medical advice.

Read Spiritual Books

A rapidly growing number of very good books are now available in paperback, filled with fascinating data, spiritual advice, provocative stories, little exercises, and a wide variety of viewpoints about things spiritual and paranormal. These can provide a continuing source of support on your own personal journey—a band of guides, advisors, and companions. They can also help protect you from becoming utterly bogged down in physical-plane activities and distractions. Many contain little exercises that anyone can do in a few spare minutes, and you can easily try some that feel right for you.

Most people seem to find the contemporary spiritual books most easily understandable and most applicable to their current lives. Many of the universal truths may be timeless, but for many they are more easily communicated through today's images. Also, current books haven't been "fiddled with" by zealots and sectarians. And, in my opinion, *Seth Speaks*, for example, is as sacred as, say, the *Tao Te Ching.*

The fact that so many books are now so inexpensively and easily available to such a large portion of the world's population is something brand new in history. It has implications that we have only begun to see. The Recommended Readings section at the end of this book contains a list of works that I and others have found exciting and enlightening. Enjoy!

The books themselves will begin to shift your perspective in a more positive, expansive direction. Just reading books can produce some good changes. But you also might want to do something, actively. You can be well read in the new perspectives and yet access only a fraction of their potential help, unless you do some practicing.

Reduce Negativity; Increase Positiveness

This is the great-great grandmother of all spiritual advice.

It's hard at first to grasp the deep extent to which we have been mentally programmed by ourselves and others, hard for us to see layers of the program patterns that are determining our life experiences. The programming exists in layers, like veils. This is why *any* progress in this area is a real gain. This is also why people sometimes get discouraged because they no sooner penetrate one layer than they find another beneath it. Self-reprogramming takes some work, but the rewards can be tremendous.

Creative Visualization writers note how most of us visualize, continuously creating our realities without realizing it. A disconcerting proportion of our self-fulfilling thoughts and mental images are negative or self-limiting. This doesn't make us "bad"; it just means we may be stuck in patterns we really don't desire. "I'm always exhausted by the end of the day." "I hate going to the dentist." "I have trouble meeting new people." "I don't think I can do it." Henry Ford said, "If you think you can, or you think you can't—you're right."

By my count, some people communicate five or six negative, discouraging, limiting remarks to themselves and others for every one that is encouraging or positive. *If we could just change these ratios we would change the world.*

It took us a long time to get to where we presently are in terms of negative and self-limiting programming, so none of us gets rid of it all in a day. But, as the fabled Chinese philosopher said, the journey of a thousand miles begins with one step. And there are plenty of improvements and lifts of the spirit possible all along the way.

The other, equally important, side of this suggestion is to reach and stretch as high as you can toward the lighter, higher vibration levels. Reach for the positives: light, love, joy, enthusiasm, warm feelings, humor, good thoughts about oneself and others, optimism, seeing the best in people and situations, seeing opportunities instead of only barriers. Cheerfulness is catching. Laughter is therapeutic. Warm feelings are pleasurable. Positive affirmations work, sometimes even against grave diseases. Never underestimate the power of either negative or positive thinking (and feeling). More than anything else, the fate of our planet may well hang on this one point.

Be as light-handed and light-hearted as you can. Hold your identity, your roles, your relationships, and your possessions lightly. Compulsions and obsessions belong to the coarser, heavier wavelengths. We are vulnerable and other-directed to the extent that we take our gender or social standing or physical appearance or name or age too seriously. All these things will shift and change; only the spirit is eternal. So look for the underlying spirit in things and other people and yourself, even if you can only catch a glimpse for now. This will help keep you tuned toward the spiritual wellsprings of all creations and manifestations.

I know—these things are easier said than done. But they are also easier done than people often think. Affirmations work! Not all at once, and often in surprising ways, but they work. When you first begin to broadcast positive affirmations, such as "I enjoy an abundance of all good things," or "I like myself," you can almost hear the realities around you creak and begin to shift gears. Repeat, repeat, repeat.

You can make a game out of positive suggestion, developing and repeating affirmations, and discovering and dissolving negative patterns. Anyone walking around seething with resentments is at risk. There is already far too much negativity in the world; the world is an echo chamber for it. Add as little as you can and erase as much as you can. The best, most straightforward book I know of dealing with this is *You Can Heal Your Life*, by Louise Hay, the lady who healed herself of terminal cancer.

Nurture Yourself: Body, Mind, and Spirit

There are many ways to be your own best friend. For starters, whatever else you are doing, see that you have some personal downtime each day when you do something you *like*, even if it can only be a few minutes. Luxuriate in a hot bath to help relax tense muscles. Take a stroll and notice the foliage and house designs around your neighborhood. Read some dumb escapist literature, if it helps you disengage for a bit. Do whatever works for you to bring some rest and play into your life. You spend time with other people, so spend some with yourself. You listen all the time to other people, so listen to yourself. You invest in retirement and major medical plans, so invest in yourself.

Some downtime often provides at least subliminal contact with the larger spiritual realms and the deeper spiritual you. Even machines are periodically taken off line to cool down.

The neglect of downtime results in an accumulation of a peculiar kind of strain and weariness that is very uncomfortable and can produce further physical and personal difficulties. Conversely, regular downtime can provide a continual refreshing and revitalizing of one's entire configuration. An employer or supervisor who is tolerant of worker downtime and silliness will get back far more than that concession costs. This is true, as well, for the self-employed.

There are some easy things we can do for the body which don't require any radical change in lifestyle, or any painful and expensive treatments. Bodies, being anchored in the physical plane, inevitably do wear out. But there are things that can be done to make living in one more comfortable. According to emerging medical research and holistic health workers, we can make good progress in detoxifying the body and restoring a better biochemical balance simply by adding some vegetables and fruits to our diet. The fruits help cleanse the body, while the leafy vegetables provide needed nutrients for body repair. Evidently, an apple a day *will* help keep the doctor away. And evidently leafy vegetables, rich in potassium and other minerals, were major ingredients in the "magic potions" prepared by women healers in the Middle Ages.

Another emerging research finding that is easy for anyone to apply is mild exercise, which can significantly contribute to health and lifespan, reducing the risks of heart attacks and other unpleasantries. Evidently, mild exercises such as housework, yardwork, or a daily stroll are as effective in this as more vigorous and demanding work-out programs.

The effects of slightly improved nutrition and exercise habits are subtle but powerful over any length of time. Health-care professionals tell us that the average person in Western society continuously carries around many pounds of feces and toxins stored in the intestinal tract, and that most modern urban people are excessively acidic because of their lifestyles. These conditions obviously do not help generate well-being. If a person felt even ten-percent better physically most of the time, other positive changes would follow. Preoccupation with bodily processes can be self-defeating, but some attention to them, like one might give to one's car, makes good sense.

With a little effort we can easily pursue simple meditation, aerobics, or some gentle form of physical yoga. The findings of recent scientific studies strongly suggest that these activities can be very helpful in reducing stress, reducing blood pressure, and alleviating other bodily ills. They also seem to help restore flexibility and stimulate the movement of nerve impulses and fluid circulation. The benefits of these kinds of practices are now being extended in programs for senior citizens and the handicapped. There are good books on these subjects (some listed in Recommended Readings) or one can attend weekly classes for modest fees in most areas.

With regard to nurturing yourself, there is a danger of "reverse discrimination"—exalting all things spiritual and belittling anything that seems mundane. This misses the fact that *everything* stems, directly or indirectly, from spirituality. It also misses the fact that we are here to experience the physical plane. Enjoying a piece of watermelon can be as spiritual as meditating. Experience it all.

Seek and Create Win-Win Games

In Game Theory, which is rapidly growing as a tool in think tanks and the burgeoning conflict-resolution profession, there are three pure outcomes to any human enterprise when treated as a game. One is Lose-Lose, an activity in which all participants lose, like a squabble among loved ones, or a nuclear war. Two is Win-Lose, in which one party's winning necessitates someone else losing, as in competitive sports or a con man and his victim. Three is Win-Win, in which all participants win, at least to some extent, from the activity. Examples: a salesman and a pleased customer, a pleasant social occasion, or a kiss between two consenting people.

When you look closely, you discover that a tremendous percentage of human activity and social life consists of either Lose-Lose or Win-Lose scenarios. Also, a great many apparently Win-Lose situations actually turn out to be Lose-Lose. How often have you really "won" in an argument—and what did you win? As the veteran New Ager, Ken Keyes Jr., likes to point out, it is much nicer to be loved than to be right.

Just being aware of the Game Theory principles sensitizes a person to how they and others are handling their endeavors. I know of a few people—a real estate broker, a dentist, a hardware store owner, an investment dealer—who operate partially on a Win-Win basis. Within a few years, they have become a legend in their own areas and have more business than they can easily handle.

It is easier when starting out with this technology for most people to create and carry out small Win-Win activities. You can very easily be friendly or complimentary to someone sharing an elevator with you for a few seconds. Or you can thank a spouse who cooked a meal. "Thank yous" are much more than a matter of politeness; they affirm the connectedness and cooperativeness in human interactions and strengthen them so that more positive interchanges can flow.

Then there's the old technique called "Wait a Second." If given a moment's chance, people will often say something like, "Sorry, I'm cranky today," after snapping at you. So give them a few seconds to correct their own course, instead of instantly flashing back. Irritability and dourness can spread through an entire interpersonal network like a flu virus, if everyone just passes it on. By simply not doing so, you can save half a dozen or more people from a contagion of negativity. And don't just give up if you sometimes fail to do so. Just think—if you succeed in *not* passing it on, say, 50 out of 100 times, what an advance that will be.

The way our present physical-plane society is rigged, it is probably impossible to avoid all Win-Lose games. But anyone can shift the balance in favor of Win-Win situations. There is a simple underlying principle at work here. Lose-Lose and Win-Lose enterprises create negative karma. Win-Win games produce positive karma. Shifting the balance therefore sweetens up not only our current living experiences, but also the upcoming millennia.

When you imaginatively put yourself in the other person's shoes to see where they're coming from, and focus on the connectedness instead of the separateness of people, it becomes much easier to come up with Win-Win scenarios. Win-Win situations can also be envisioned as rippling outward as far as possible. Many people establish Win-Win scenarios for their own family and immediate interpersonal network, but at the expense of other people outside these circles who are treated as fair game. This is certainly a beginning, and is preferable to utter self-centeredness. But it continues to perpetuate divisiveness among humans.

Self-sacrifice, where you lose so that others can win, is not a good game either. Don't just "be nice" in shy appeasement, giving up your desires, or a promotion, or a spouse, to someone else. Lose-Win is still a Win-Lose outcome.

Without much awareness of our interconnectedness as beings, and with undeveloped empathy, we often perpetrate a stream of small cruelties and thoughtlessness upon one another. We frequently have our feelings hurt and we frequently hurt others when we don't mean to. Developing the habit of creating even small Win-Win actions can help alleviate this somewhat chronic social condition.

Doing For Others

What can we do for others? Less than we would like to, sometimes, but more than we often realize. Over the years, I've noticed some strange things on the subject of helping others, and I've learned some lessons, mostly the hard way. As the channeled, advanced spirit, Michael, has said, it's a good thing to open doors for people, but not good to try to shove them through the doors.

I vividly remember many instances when I thought I knew best what someone needed or what someone should do. In a very few cases I was "right," but most of the time I was simply trying to foist my own viewpoints and assessments and priorities (and zealousness) upon others, with little understanding of *their* world or *their* path.

In seeking to help others, we often subconsciously attempt to impose our own viewpoints and desires, and to manipulate them into alignment with us. There are examples of this everywhere. Some people don't respond to medical treatments or tearful entreaties from relatives, because they are ready to move on to their own stage of development. Clutching at them in the hope that they will remain on the physical plane is certainly understandable—but it is no help to them. Or, a teenager might not be turning out the way parents deeply desire—but who does that life belong to? People *need* to walk their own path. If this path diverges sharply from ours and we are emotionally tied to them, we may spend huge amounts of effort to persuade them to "mend their ways," but to no avail. The only results will be upset, frustration, and estrangement. It seems that one of the hardest lessons to learn is to just let people walk their own path and to assist them on *their* road. People who have cats often learn something of this lesson. You can't "own" a cat, but you can have an intense, mutually supportive, mutually enriching relationship with one.

What we can do for (or to) others becomes much clearer when we begin to view the cosmos around us as comprised of holograms of vibrational fields. *In truth, we can't refrain from influencing others since we are part of their fields*. In our continuous interactions with others, both physical and psychic, we emanate healing or dis-ease. As Mentor/Meredith Lady Young points out in her fascinating book, *Agartha*, all human beings are potential healers. Love energies, for instance, literally neutralize blockages and negativities in our own and others' bodies. As we manifest ourselves, we can literally be a boon or a pain (in any part of the body) to others.

Beyond this, we can go on to assist those who ask. With or without being asked, we can also help provide opportunities for other people's life-development. We often can facilitate their growth possibilities; we can show options, and communicate the things we have learned in a non-coercive way. We can let others be themselves. (Remember how precious a friendship is when you can just be yourself?) We can work to release other people from our grudges and resentments, and they will feel some relief whether they consciously recognize it or not. Can we make a difference for others? We sure can! In *Emmanuel's Book* (compiled by Pat Rodegast and Judith Stanton), Emmanuel points out that all of our actions, including our thoughts, create ripples that spread out endlessly.

Spiritual writers seem to agree that, ideally, help should be given unconditionally, with no strings attached, no self-glorification, and no indebtedness incurred. This is an ideal, not altogether easy to achieve, but worth reaching toward. Why? Well, it turns out that this is far more than a piece of morality. The people who continually do this are getting their kicks all day long. Such unconditional helping activities are extremely pleasurable in and of themselves. As an added bonus, they build up our positive karmic bank account. We end up having friends all over the cosmos. Believe it or not, we already do.

It seems that helping *any* consciousness is as important and worthy as helping any other. The timorous youth or quiet, submissive secretary of today may be the Gandhi or the Mother Teresa of an upcoming century. Tending seeds or tending saplings is as valuable as tending tall willows or giant oaks.

Keep Going

There is always something you can do to help yourself grow and learn from experience, to become lighter and more positive, no matter how poor or pressed you might be right now. Take charge of your own consciousness evolvement; don't leave it in the hands of others. Laugh. Celebrate even the "smaller" things.

There will be good days and bad, backslides, interpersonal network flareups, negativities, toxins stirred up, and so on. But there will also be some signs of change and transformation, such as noticing natural beauty for a moment, feeling a bit of welcome peacefulness, experiencing some warm sensations in your energy centers, enjoying a spontaneous smile from an unlikely person, easing of blockage and barriers in relationships, remembering wisps of an astral dream experience, or relishing a fleeting spiritual contact with another being.

All the things mentioned in this chapter are simple and basic. Yet these alone can transform a life and impel you toward spiritual awakening. As Orin/Sanaya Roman points out, any progress you make opens the way and makes it easier for all those one step behind you. Maybe that is the ultimate Win-Win game of them all.

17

Beneath The New Age

There are things going on today that are brand new in history. They have never happened before, at least not on this planet. As eminent sociologist Ian Robertson, and world famous physicist Fritjof Capra, and visionary theologian Teilhard de Chardin, and so many others have documented, almost every area of our society is in a state of transition. We are entering a post-industrial or information age. Three-fourths of the world's people will soon be urban dwellers and we are reaching a population density never before experienced. Diffusion between societies of new discoveries and ideas, and of new social ills, such as AIDS, is more swift and massive than ever before. Our manipulation of all facets of the environment is at an all-time high. Through television, over seven hundred million people now sometimes simultaneously watch the same events. Literacy rates worldwide are far higher than in any previous epoch. The world's currencies and economies float against one another with little or no solid anchorage. And the human potential movement has turned conventional psychology on its head.

For better or worse, we are currently in the midst of a historical transition into a new era. It's a new ball game. The old days are gone, and most experts agree that we don't quite know what we're doing in these new days. This is the background for the New Age movement.

So, what is this "New Age"? The term "New Age," like the earlier terms "hippie" and "yuppie," is partly an accurate designation and partly a mass media stereotype, a symbolic canopy beneath which a very wide variety of phenomena are thrown. There is *something* going on, everyone agrees, but what? Well, beyond the hype and buzzwords, a real spiritual movement is occurring in this country and throughout the world. Traces of this movement are everywhere if one wants to look. Every week now, I hear about another group or activity or institute involved in things spiritual, and they are scattered throughout the entire Western hemisphere.

Within the movement, there are more things going on than any single person could ever possibly keep track of. "The New Age" is a generality that has so many separate strands they can hardly be counted. There are groups of people working independently, perhaps not even knowing of one another, but heading in similar directions. Because it is so vast and many-stranded, no one person or organization can speak for the entire movement. No one book, including this one, can cover it all.

The widespread confusion about the New Age seems to arise from the fact that it includes so many paths and activities. For starters, there seem to be two levels or strata to the movement: a glitzy, extravagant surface level, and beneath this, a quieter, less advertised level. The faddish surface level of the movement has brought out the hucksters, the profiteers, the thrill seekers, and the deluded. A carnival, complete with spiritual barkers and jugglers and clowns. The level of genuine spiritual awakening is quieter and deeper and more powerful, and still a bit underground. The populace has not been very well informed and so they can have trouble distinguishing between these two. But don't be misled. The underlying level is for real. Its roots are as strong as the cosmic tides and run as deep as the deathless soul. The problem of charlatans, hypes, and exploiters is not going to go away. But the movement is growing up as well as growing.

With few exceptions, the media coverage of the New Age has been awesomely inept. As Jeremy Tarcher, the publisher of many New Age books, has pointed out, you wouldn't send someone who knows nothing about football to cover the Super Bowl. Yet the reporters sent to cover the New Age have usually known little or nothing about metaphysics, alternative health traditions, leading-edge science, the occult, or any of the other underpinnings of the movement. And they have focused only on the bizarre and faddish aspects that make for catchy headlines. They've simply missed the story.

So what is the story? Instead of dropping names and collecting pro and con quotes, we can analyze the New Age as a "social movement," using some of the tools of psychology and sociology. When we do this, many aspects come into better focus.

The New Age has become a national controversy that breaks down into hundreds of thousands of individual controversies all over the country. At the dinner table, a wife says she is fascinated by New Age ideas and she's always liked Shirley MacLaine, and her husband tells her, "They're all crazy." Without reading any of the literature, a doctor dismisses NDEs and out-of-body reports and warns his patients about them, while a head nurse is converted by the stories she hears in the recovery room. A psychiatrist dismisses all such experiences as neurological, and quotes some founding psycho-father, while one of his colleagues takes up the practice of past-life regression almost as a new career. One minister condemns it as a sign of the Antichrist, while the minister down the block takes up spiritual healing and Creative Visualization techniques. A television comedian does a routine that includes some funny and disparaging jokes about the New Age. Two youths watching the show laugh heartily, but subsequently one of them begins to check it out. Meanwhile, another well-known television figure publicly states that he has been helped through many life situations by his spirit guides. A surgeon writes a widely read book theorizing about the biological basis for alleged altered states of consciousness. Another surgeon writes a bestseller about the spiritual miracles he has personally witnessed in the operating room.

All of these individual controversies arise, in part, because of the amorphousness of the spiritual movement itself. The movement seems amorphous because it *is* amorphous. It has no hierarchical leadership

centralized organization. So it is not an "or-
ment, in any ordinary sense of the word. There are
upon hundreds of little organizations and thousands of
informal groups scattered throughout the country. There are a
few hundred individuals whose names are somewhat well known in some sectors of the movement, because of their work as writers, researchers, or spiritual practitioners, or often all three. Many of these practitioners influence some groups in the movement, but none of them is accepted by them all. So the movement is almost the ultimate in democratic decentralization and amorphousness, collectively created and "owned" only by the large number of participants.

In a sense, the amorphousness of the movement is its very strength. There's no single leader or organization that can be discredited or taken out. It shares with wind and water the property of diffuseness. For example, while some Establishment authority figure is busily denouncing past-life regression therapy, someone, somewhere else, is publishing a book on out-of-body experiences or the healing results of opening blocked energy flows through the chakras. A would-be oppressor doesn't know which way to turn. This might possibly become a vital point in upcoming decades.

As with any large social movement, the various "wings" or vectors of the New Age differ from one another in how extensively they diverge from mainstream conventional society—on how far out they are. These wings vary in their positions on everything from nutrition to flying saucers. Some, like most academic parapsychologists, are only one step beyond the conventional. Others are so esoteric in their beliefs and activities that they defy easy description, as for example, some schools of shamanism and witchcraft. Each wing tends to have at least a nodding acquaintance with, and a surprising degree of tolerance for, many of the others. Despite their many differences, there is some sense of camaraderie, because they virtually all share a consensus that it is time for a change. And they share similar underlying goals of spiritual growth.

There are some distinctive regional differences in the movement. The East Coast has more of an intellectual and "scientific" flavor, with influences from early American transcendentalists and European occult traditions. The West Coast has much more of an Eastern flavor, more emotional immediacy, California lotus land touches, and some hang-loose echoes from the sixties. The Midwest and South are much closer to traditional Judeo-Christian concepts and middle-of-the-road American values, but with a strong supernatural slant and a kind of homespun spiritualism that is taken seriously. In England, Europe and Latin America, the movement reflects some aspects of those regional societies. In Central America and Brazil, for instance, native traditions are at the forefront of spiritual awakening. Although the words and symbolic interpetations differ somewhat from region to region, they all seem to share the basic emergent themes presented in Chapter One. How many of those involved would apply the label "New Age" to themselves is an open question. But they are demonstrably involved in a spiritual movement.

All age groups are involved with the movement. Frequently a couple or an entire family will be involved together. In terms of percentages, those in the mid-life period and beyond are the majority, but one can find plenty of young kids, youths, and very senior citizens.

Both sexes are well represented, and there is more equality and less sexism than you find in most current mainstream societies. In fact, there seem to be as many influential females as males in New Age groups.

In terms of social class, there are far more members from the upper and middle classes than the working and lower classes. This may be partly a matter of time and resources. Civilization has always been in part a matter of available leisure time.

In racial and ethnic composition, WASPS (white, Anglo-Saxon Protestants) clearly predominate. Only a few blacks, Latinos, and American Indians are involved, as a scan of the audience at any spiritual seminar or the customers in a New Age bookstore will quickly confirm.

This fact will need to be addressed, lest humanity remain divided.

Exact figures for all of these broad characteristics are, of course, impossible to know. These are only careful estimates, checked against the impressions of others who have "been around."

How large is the spiritual movement? We have seen that the percentages of Americans who believe in reincarnation, who feel they have communicated with disembodied spirits, or who report profound paranormal experiences, have significantly increased in recent years. The number of consciousness-raising seminars and psychic newsletters has also dramatically increased. The shelf space taken up by New Age books in major chain bookstores has expanded. Even the fact that some Establishment religious leaders and conventional scientific authorities have felt it necessary to speak out against the movement attests to its growth. Johnny Carson acknowledges Shirley MacLaine's number-one bestselling book, *Going Within*, by joking about it, and very conventional department stores are selling crystals. But this is only part of the story.

Surrounded by companions and enthusiastic acquaintances, it is easy for those who are deeply involved to overestimate the size, strength, and breadth of the movement. They tend to presume that the flurry of activities they are personally involved in is going on everywhere. On the other hand, mainstream people who are uninvolved and disbelieving tend to greatly underestimate how much is going on, and may dismiss it all as a "fringie" fad. Not surprisingly, the truth is somewhere in between.

A major social movement clearly is going on, but it is still something of a fringe movement which has not fully penetrated mainstream societies. The New Age seems to be in about the same position of rock-and-roll or science fiction during the late fifties: widely, if somewhat defensively, supported, but still rather disreputable in the eyes of conventional society, and periodically denounced by some of the culture's authorities. There is still an intimidation factor at work although it is weakening. Many people involved in things spiritual are still careful about who they talk to and what they say. This will continue to some extent as long as spirituality is a minority movement rather than an established and accepted part of most peoples' lives.

There is no simple answer to the question of how many people are active in the New Age movement, because people are involved in so many different ways and degrees. We can get a clearer picture if we address the question in terms of circles of degree of involvement, ranging from intense to incidental. In the innermost circle there are some tens of thousands of people for whom the spiritual movement is their profession and/or their ruling passion. These people live, breathe, and work in the New Age to a large extent, and decide their lifestyle priorities accordingly. They form something of a community, and most of their friends, acquaintances, and lovers are drawn from the ranks of fellow enthusiasts. Marilyn Ferguson may be correct in calling them "conspirators," because they do just about anything they can to further the movement, hoping and working toward the day when the majority of the world's population "catches the spirit." It is interesting that they are more kindly and compassionate toward the rest of society than society is toward them.

Beyond these, there is a circle of some hundreds of thousands of people who are actively pursuing consciousness expansion and spiritual growth in some form or other. For many of these, mundane career and family commitments prevent their full-time involvement, but their hearts are in the movement. They follow many varieties of spiritual self-development, from leading-edge psychological approaches to rarified transcendental paths, and many would not call themselves New Age people. But they share a sense of being involved in "something big," as one lady put it. They are the steady customers at New Age bookstores and workshops, and the steady clients of spiritual practitioners.

In the next circle outward are some few million people who have a sporadic but real interest in things spiritual. These form the numerical bulk of the book buyers and seminar attendees, the curious shoppers at psychic fairs and the interested listeners to paranormal stories. They accept that there are spiritual aspects to humans, and spiritual things going on in the cosmos, but tend to be skeptical about the claims of the more far-out wings. In many cases they have had direct conscious paranormal experiences, and are mulling over what these may have meant.

Members of this circle usually have many physical-plane concerns and preoccupations, which keep them well grounded in the mundane world while they poke and sift around in more arcane matters. The individuals in this circle vary greatly in their degree of spiritual savvy, and some are vulnerable to cult persuasions or psychic con games. But they form a very important part of the movement.

Among them are the nurses and ministers who listen with some understanding to the out-of-body experiences of their patients and parishioners. They include the friends and acquaintances who are open-minded and supportive of someone's ESP experiences. They tell others in their network about a fascinating New Age book they have read. They are the quiet defenders of the Shirley MacLaines and the Jane Robertses and the guy at the office who is into yoga. If their hearts are not so light, neither are they so closed and heavy as those entirely focused on the physical plane. In attitude and sheer numbers, they form a collective, supporting, vibrational cushion both for members of the inner circles of involvement and for newcomers beginning on their paths.

Beyond this group there is a final circle of some tens of millions of individuals who have had a few "funny experiences," or who hold tentative beliefs that there is something to these spiritual assertions. Their conscious knowledge about such matters usually is superficial or virtually nonexistent. So they may take the word of their minister or a popular journalist on paranormal questions that come up. Because of this, their beliefs about things spiritual waver back and forth, to some extent, with the opinions they encounter. They are likely to have been Star Trek or Twilight Zone fans; they may have seen Shirley MacLaine's miniseries, but not have read her book; they may check their daily horoscope in the newspaper, "just for fun".

Their acceptance of spiritual assertions is partial, conditional, and selective. For instance, they may accept the validity of ESP, but have strong doubts about reincarnation. Or they may believe that we "go somewhere" after we die, but reject the notion that their house plants and pets have their own forms of consciousness. In some manner they have been touched by spirituality, and something in them has resonated in response, although they may not know quite what to make of it. In many ways they resemble the large category of "undecided" voters in a political election. They exist as a very important, but uncommitted potential.

Each of these circles is growing in numbers. And there is a steady progression of people inward: an uncommitted person moves into the active, part-time circle, and so on. There doesn't appear to be much movement back outward, although an active person will sometimes go through periods of needing to focus on mundane concerns. But once a person has experienced some awakening, it seems that even the most mundane situations are handled in a more spiritual manner.

The spiritual awakening movement is a creative new fusion of root elements from Eastern and Western cultures. Both traditions have contributed strengths, and each has helped balance some weaknesses inherent in the other. So the amalgamation can legitimately be termed "New" Age, since the blend is fresh and unique. To put it oversimply, the East has contributed a vaulting mysticism and a great deal of data about spiritual aspects of the cosmos; while the West has contributed the scientific method and empirical rules of evidence, and an emphasis on practical workability. But there is much more to it.

Many individuals who have chosen some spiritual path have embraced an Eastern way. In some instances, they extoll the virtues of the East and derogate the West for its crass materialism, sterile logic, and inhuman scientism that exalts deductive thinking and downgrades intuition. True, it is fairly easy to take potshots at the West (while taking comfort in its benefits). Not surprisingly, some in the West have held an opposite view: that the East is far too impractical and other-worldly. They want workable, active principles that can be verified and refined, not obscure parables one can eternally ponder. Meanwhile, as Shakti Gawain has observed, in the urban areas of India we have Westerners buying metaphysical artifacts and Easterners buying jeans and transistor radios.

In evaluating the traditions of East and West, we should look at some hard facts. It's true that the East has been the birthplace of some of the most transcendental documents and spiritual teachers in the history of this planet. But many of these documents are dogma ridden. And the lands of Asia are chock full of poverty, ignorance, stark class and sex discrimination, cruelty and inhumanity aplenty. Ancient and current history demonstrates that many people in these lands have all the spiritual sensitivity of a tree sloth and all the compassion of a stormtrooper.

Meanwhile, much of the West has become utterly entranced with secular outward forms and gimmicks. As the theosophist Leadbetter noted, Westerners are prone to say they have a soul, as if it were some vague appendage, and let it go at that.

We can talk as long as we wish about the best and the worst of each tradition. It is easy to overrate the spirituality of the East and underrate the spirituality of the West. In the West, spiritual traditions have tended to go underground, partly because they have often been repressed by the prevailing organized religions. In the East, spirituality has almost always been more open, partly because aspects of it were often co-opted and used for political purposes by the ruling classes. (No—you won't come back as a pig if you displease your masters.) Needless to say, each of these historical situations has led to distortions of an original high spiritual impulse.

On the whole, the New Age movement does not cling overmuch to either tradition. Instead, it rather audaciously borrows and creatively adapts ingredients from each, to form a truly new recipe.

Kipling once penned the famous lines that "East is East and West is West, and never the twain shall meet." It turns out that he was wrong. They have met, they have crossbred, and they have an offspring. But the "parents" aren't altogether sure they want the child.

What's *new* about the New Age Movement? Although some of its roots are ancient, it represents a new synthesis, just as water is a new substance that differs markedly from its original components of hydrogen and oxygen. For example, the current fusion of scientific empiricism with mysticism certainly seems new, and is now providing more refined, verifiable data on spiritual matters than we have ever had before. There are many areas where science and religion are now overlapping, as in the studies of near-death experiences, the links between brain-wave patterns and altered states of consciousness, the photographic documentation of auras and healing energies, empirical studies on the power of prayer, and so on. The feats of yoga masters and child prodigies are now being videotaped for anyone to see. I strongly suspect such developments are really just getting started.

The marriage of elements from our post-industrial mass society with elements of consciousness expansion is also producing some developments that are brand new in history. For instance, a new paperback book on reincarnation or advice from spirit guides can spread through the entire Western world in a matter of months. Or tens of millions of people can simultaneously see a television miniseries or talk show on the paranormal. Events and trends move much more swiftly now. Increasingly sophisticated biofeedback machines and meditation cassettes are being mass produced and mass marketed. Telephones, computer networks, and swift mail delivery can now quickly and easily link those in the movement who are geographically separated but like-minded in interests. These facts may seem obvious, but don't overlook the fact that mass communication of spiritual matters on this scale is *new*, and long-term implications can only be guessed at. Certainly it is speeding things up. The rapid, worldwide growth of the spiritual awakening movement would have been impossible without these technological developments.

Civilizations are not always user-friendly, as we have seen. Both the East and the West have had cultural patterns which have often impoverished the lives of their peoples. The West has had a prevailing tradition of individualism and self-reliance while the East has emphasized a web of close-knit families and communities. Each tradition has its merits but also its minus side. A close-knit interpersonal web can submerge and smother an individual even as it supports him or her. In the West, our urban "looseness" leads to a good deal of personal freedom. But, without some spirituality, it can also leave us adrift, lonely, separated, and alienated. Neither a plodding subordinated life with few personal choices nor a sour drifting life among strangers seems very attractive.

New Agers are proving that these two polarities of individualism and togetherness are neither in conflict with each other nor mutually exclusive. They are doing this professionally and in their own personal lives. Both self-realization and the interconnectedness of all things are manifested in the major teachings and techniques, with growth in spiritual awareness being the bridge. The integration of these two poles holds the promise of resolving an imbalance which has dogged humanity's footsteps since the beginning of history. And it would have important side-effects such as the mellowing of interpersonal relationships and increased direct awareness of our environment.

Are there blind spots in the New Age movement? Yes. After all, the movement is being carried out by human beings who are themselves still in the throes of evolution on the physical plane. There are the hypes which are fairly frequent on the superficial level of the movement. Each month I receive several advertisements and come-ons in the mail which offer to use the stars, or the number of letters in my name, or an alleged contact with the Lords of the Galaxy, to help me win the lottery or get laid—for a price. But I receive comparable come-ons in the mail from coin salesmen, credit card companies, college diploma mills, retirement counsellors, mail-order investment firms, and one-day sales. The serious seeker learns to sort through all this silliness. The sad thing is that these kinds of ads tarnish the reputation of the entire movement for some people by slandering what is really going on.

Blind spots. Many New Agers seem to grossly underestimate how locked-in and stuck in their ways the majority of human beings are; how much tunnel vision and inertia there is in their lives. Even those who work professionally to release addictions often seem to be innocent about the depths of such addictions. Spending some time teaching in a midwestern high school or living in a rustbelt city would be sobering. It would be wonderful if all of humanity could be uplifted through a short talk on positive thinking, but it proves not to be that quick or easy. The entrenched inertia of humanity can be awesome. But, I have the sneaking suspicion that the collective enthusiasm and skill of the New Agers will sooner or later carry the day.

Another blind spot seems to be the movement's unwillingness to face up to "evil." From a cosmic perspective, it may be entirely true that evil is merely the result of ignorance and only a temporary shadow along the way in the evolutionary process. But you'll have a hard time convincing someone of this when their teenage child has been brutally murdered or when they are withering away in a Third World political prison. These subjects are painful, and it is unhealthy to dwell upon them overmuch. It is healthier to accentuate the positive. But to say, "Well, it's all for the best. It's what they need, and part of the perfect plan," as some New Age writers have, can be seriously superficial and naive. I can grasp the idea that Hitler might be my friend a couple of millennia down the road, but for now, I'm certainly not going to vote for him.

Many areas of our planet are still very barbarous, and there are many other areas where the spiritual light is dim. There are now over five billion humans living on our planet. From our best demographic data, two-thirds of these individuals are living more or less downtrodden lives. Most of the people in modernized, industrial countries are doing rather well. But life in many other areas of the globe is so stark that we don't want to hear about it. As a species, we all share a collective karma involving all of humanity. We each had a hand in creating this karma, and will each have a hand in clearing up and transcending it. This, too, must be taken into account in planning and dreaming for a New Age.

So we're coming into a new world and the New Age movement is one of the main catalysts. A lot is going on. But let me tell you what I think is really going on, beneath all the New Age words and images and debates.

Everyone who stirs or awakens spiritually alters the collective vibrational patterns of the planet, thereby lightening the intensity of the Earth trance with its concentration of coarser wavelengths. This makes it easier for the next person to awaken. It is a lovely progression that holds true for a group, a locale, a country, the entire world, and even the lower astral planes. As this process continues, it eventually reaches the point where it becomes difficult for anyone to remain asleep.

18

The Vision

What does all this really amount to? you might ask. Is the spiritual awakening movement having any real or lasting influence? Is it going anywhere? In the last two decades, millions of copies of books on consciousness expansion and spiritual awareness have been bought. Hundreds of thousands of people have attended a variety of spiritual workshops, virtually all of which have offered workable techniques for self-development and the betterment of the world. So why no Golden Age? Why hasn't the world been transformed?

Well, the world has been changed! To what degree we will never know, because there's no way to assess what the last few decades *would have been without such influences to lighten things up.* Who knows? —the millions of people praying and meditating for peace may have poured forth enough positive energies to have prevented the World War Three that so many had predicted.

How many people are happier because someone poured loving and healing energies toward them, or successfully worked through something karmic that was tying both of them down? How many lives have been enriched, or even saved, through some tendril of the movement? To what degree have all the recent gloom-and-doom scenarios been softened or even sidestepped because of the spiritual awakening of a few million people? Such leavening effects may well be far greater than any of us yet realize. They may have been saving the world all along.

Here's a curious incident. The "Harmonic Convergence" ceremonies, held at various sacred spots across the country on August 16th, 1987, were derisively laughed at both privately and publicly by the rest of the nation. Based on some alleged conjunctions from a

Mayan calendar, they were a national joke. But, immediately afterward, a cowboy president of the United States and a tough Russian leader who had risen through the ranks and survived years of Kremlin politics began to work intensively on international disarmament and the easing of world tensions. Coincidence? I don't know.

Where is the New Age movement trying to get to? What is its "vision"? The answer seems to be nothing less than world transformation. The collective intuition is that we already have the technology, both physical and spiritual, to reduce the tragedies of this world to a very small fraction of what they presently are.

Transformation and abundance. The idea of abundance can be startling at first because we've been fed so much on the idea of scarcity. But if you look around with lifted eyes, you can see abundance everywhere throughout our universe. Ecologists tell us that, except for political and economic barriers, our planet can easily feed all of its peoples. We created these barriers and we can dismantle them. And we can choose to heal the Earth.

Our current world situations are seen as a transition time that will be as smooth or rough as we choose to make it. Beyond this time of tumult there is the glimpsed possibility of a very different pattern of life, in which widespread expanded consciousness will have transformed every aspect of our physical and social arrangements into much more luxuriant forms. In other words, the world can become much more user-friendly.

By its very nature, you can't force enlightenment on anyone. But you can provide surroundings that are either stark and grim or beautiful and adventurous. The New Age envisions a world in which people can have the physical and spiritual raw materials to reach their full potentials if they so choose.

After thousands of hours of counseling and teaching, I have become convinced that most people over the age of two are among the walking wounded. Nor are their physical, psychological, and spiritual wounds to be healed by a change in presidents or the new fall televison season. The sceneries and the props of our lives must be altered, and some new scripts made available on a mass basis, for real and lasting transformations to occur. If you buy almost anyone a coffee or a drink and listen to their stories, you'll see what I mean.

People *want* visions that hold some promise of uplifting and going forward. To paraphrase the famous author, W. Somerset Maughm: the hell with the critics; people like happy endings and what's wrong with that?

When I look at world trends as a sociologist, it is my own deep conviction that the Spiritual Awakening movement is the most positive, compassionate, and liberating force at work on this planet today. This thousand-legged movement is looking at the ills of the world and what is "normal" and "abnormal" from a spiritual perspective. From this vantage point, each of our problems seems to be, underneath everything else, a reflection of a lack of spirituality. The remedy? World transformation can occur simply through the contagion of spiritual awakening.

A silly dream? Perhaps. But it sure beats the alternatives.

Epilogue

Brief Chat With a Discarnate Companion

There are no final curtains in the living cosmos.
The play goes on. And the end of something
is always the beginning of something else.

Recommended Reading

These recommended books obviously reflect some of my own predispositions as well as my own current level of spiritual development. But the list is not just thrown together. It is carefully drawn from many hundreds of titles in the hope of saving you a good deal of time and effort which I and others have gone through. I've included a brief description of each book to help you in your own choosing.

I have avoided books that are too syrupy or too technical or too questionable. Undoubtedly there are many good books I've missed, and other good books will continue to appear. But each of those listed will still be well worth reading a decade from now. No one book can give you the full story, but each of them can help.

None of these authors are hucksters. All of their books represent serious work and are not just tossed off to capitalize on a faddish market. They are "veterans," who know about wounds as well as healings.

All of the books are inexpensive, either mass or trade paperback. You could buy the lot of them for the price of a weekend jaunt. Sometimes they are hard to find, but your local bookstore will probably be glad to order them for you.

If a particular book doesn't feel right or interest you right now, don't throw it away. Half a year later it may be the one that most resonates with you. Many people have found this happening again and again.

If these books were more widely read, they would significantly change our schoolbooks, our social climate, and our civilization. What more could you ask of a reading list?

The list is in intuitive order.

Very Highly Recommended

Heading Toward Omega, Kenneth Ring Ph.D., William Morrow, 1985. The definitive study of Near Death Experiencers, with extensive quotes and follow-ups. Very solidly grounded in scientific research, yet spiritually vaulting in its scope and implications for a changing worldview.

Seth Speaks, Jane Roberts, Bantam, 1972. Many have missed this book because of its plain title, but it contains enthralling discussions of physical and spiritual reality, the astral planes, between-lives choices, sleep adventures, and the properties of the soul.

You Can Heal Your Life, Louise Hay, Hay House, 1984. Put simply, this book has saved many lives and enriched many more. Topnotch manual on releasing negativities and resentments, and on using affirmations to shape your life.

Far Journeys, Robert Monroe, Dolphin, 1985. This has got to be the *Dune* of New Age writings. Reports by Monroe and his Explorer Teams on out-of-body journeys to a great variety of astral locales, and communications with many different discarnate spirits. Touches upon everything from life on the astral planes, to sexual addictions, to other-dimensional reality systems, to how we got here, to probable Earth futures. An epic, perhaps one of the most important books of our generation.

Love, Medicine & Miracles, Bernie Siegel, M.D., Harper and Row, 1986. One of the most important books on the influence of negative and positive beliefs upon disease and upon life ever written. Wonderful case illustrations of half the points in my book. A must for every social worker and health professional. Also a must if someone in your family is under treatment, if you are scheduled for an operation, or if you are planning to become ill.

Messages From Michael, Chelsea Quinn Yarbro, Berkeley, 1979. Michael is comparable to Seth as a highly evolved spirit who offers extensive data on the various evolvement stages of souls, the functions of reincarnation, life on the physical plane, and many other arcane topics. Cosmic humor too. Michael doesn't hold your hand, but he doesn't leave you in the dark either. One of my favorite books.

Eye of the Centaur, Barbara Hand Clow, Bear & Co., 1986. Far above most ordinary books on past-life journeys, because the author portrays times of illumination and transcendence as well as the influences of past traumas. The superb, long Introduction by therapist Gregory Paxson is worth the price of the book by itself. Ms. Clow has all chakras open in her accounts.

A Conscious Person's Guide to Relationships, Ken Keyes Jr., Living Love Publications, 1979. One of the wisest, yet most practical and grounded books ever written on interpersonal relationships. Keyes is fully aware of the intermix of consciousness, daily life, and the glands.

Recommended

Creative Visualization, Shakti Gawain, Bantam New Age, 1978. A practical, sweetly written book giving the essentials of easy-to-use Creative Visualization techniques. The best book I know of on the subject.

Reliving Past Lives, Helen Wambach, Harper and Row Perennial, 1978. Summarizes over eleven hundred cases of past-life regressions, providing massive statistical verification of reincarnation. Lively and provocative.

The Evolutionary Journey, Barbara Marx Hubbard, Evolutionary Press, 1982. A visionary portrayal of the evolution of human consciousness and the dawning transformation to global spirituality by one of the world's leading futurists.

Opening to Channel, Sanaya Roman and Duane Packer, H. J. Kramer, 1987. The book for anyone wishing to channel their own spirit guides or higher self. Worth reading anyway.

Astral Travel, Gavin and Yvonne Frost, Samuel Weiser, 1982. The most easily understood, scintillating presentation of the techniques and wonders of out-of-body astral travel I've run across. Delightfully pagan flavor.

Natural ESP, Ingo Swann, Bantam New Age, 1987. A very clear-headed, up-to-date presentation of laboratory ESP experiments, with many original breakthroughs and some procedures anyone can do.

Megabrain, Michael Hutchinson, Ballantine, 1986. Summarizes recent and startling scientific studies on the nature and functions of the brain, and blows away a host of fixed ideas in the process. Also contains extensive coverage of the new "mind machines" being developed for consciousness alteration.

Gentle Yoga, Lorna Bell and Eudora Seyfer, Celestial Arts, 1987. The authors have done what seemed to be the impossible—they have produced a simple, easy to understand yoga manual which anyone can use, whatever shape or state of health they are in. Beautiful job.

Agartha: A Journey to the Stars, Meredith Lady Young, Stillpoint, 1984. A channeled book with much fascinating data on vibrational energy, health, nature spirits, the Earth School scene, and easy exercises to assist spiritual development.

The Aquarian Conspiracy, Marilyn Ferguson, Jeremy P. Tarcher, 1980. A landmark book depicting the transformations currently taking place in various sectors of our society. Ms. Ferguson's erudition is awesome.

Letters From Janice, Wayne Hatford, Uni*Sun, 1987. Fascinating untutored messages from a spirit newly arrived in the Beyond, with much good data on the realities of the astral planes. A superb Afterward by Tam Mossman, the Seth books editor.

Vibrational Medicine, Richard Gerber M.D., Bear & Co., 1988. This is the book that could help transform our woeful medical scene and bring healing back into the field. A must for any health professional.

Crystal Clear, Connie Church, Villard, 1987. A simple, practical elucidation of crystals, their story and their uses. Unencumbered with metaphysical overgrowth.

Spirit Guides: We Are Not Alone, Iris Belhayes, A.C.S., 1985. An enthralling book, depicting spirit guides and their roles in our lives, the spirit worlds, and how we can help distressed spirits.

2150 A.D., Thea Alexander, Warner, 1976. Futuristic novel about how the world and human existence might transform as a result of worldwide consciousness expansion.

About The Author

J.L. Simmons, Ph.D. is the author of *Deviants* (1969) and *It's Happening: A Portrait of the Youth Scene Today*, an evaluation of 1960s youth which sold over 200,000 copies. He has done extensive field research in the areas of youth culture, personal relationships, deviancy, and spiritual pathways. In conjunction with his spiritual research, he is currently working on two more books: *Future Lives* (Bear & Company, 1990), a study of the planetary transition to a new historical spiral; and *Soul Mirrors*, a docudrama of an awakening old soul. Dr. Simmons is currently a visiting professor of sociology at the University of Missouri/St. Louis and a practicing social psychologist. He is also happily married, has two sons, and is an avid cat lover.

To Write to the Author

The author appreciates hearing from readers. Your comments are welcomed and valued. He cannot guarantee that every letter written to him will be answered, but all will be forwarded to him. Please enclose a self-addressed, stamped envelope for reply, or include $1.00 to cover costs. Write to:

J.L. Simmons
c/o Bear & Company
P.O. Drawer 2860
Santa Fe, New Mexico 87504